PRAISE

What a well-done educational resource to guide us through the Advent season! Christmas is the celebration of Christ's birth, and *It Took A Lamb* reminds us that as Christians, we must not only celebrate His birth but also never forget why He came to Earth—to die for us. Cummings and Hanberry point out that even with the very words *Merry Christmas*, "...we are actually remembering His sacrificial death as we celebrate His birth."

—Nan Kelley, Former Miss Mississippi and GAC Television Host

Drs. Scott Hanberry and Ray Cummings get it. They get it because they have spent a lifetime studying it. They get it because they have invested decades in preaching it. That is why I heartily recommend to you *It Took a Lamb*. Written by two pastor-theologians, *It Took a Lamb* is a rich resource for you to use to grasp the true meaning of the birth of Messiah during the Advent season.

—Dr. Ryan Whitley, Pastor CrossPoint Church, Trussville, AL

Something about music makes our hearts tender, fertile ground. The songs of Geron and Becky Davis have been an intricate part of my spiritual journey and worship. This devotional, *It Took a Lamb*, is an immersive act of worship that is now a part of my time with God.

—Judy Martin Hess, The Martins

Faith is defined biblically as "the substance of things hoped for, and evidence of things not seen." In an ever-changing world, we don't often hear the words *hope* and *evidence* mentioned in the same sentence. *It Took a Lamb* gives both a biblical and applicable narrative of those two influential and life-changing words. Dr. Cummings and Dr. Hanberry are not only incredible preachers and local leaders but also men who can paint a portrait through the Word of God, which may make your Christmas in this season of your life even more meaningful. Going to be good!!

—**Mitchell Williams, Fellowship of Christian Athletes**

A connecting thread of the Old and New Testaments has always created a beautiful tapestry of a lamb. Hanberry and Cummings have crafted a simple yet purposeful 41-day journey that will paint the complete picture of how Jesus was the sacrificial Lamb of God. I encourage you to incorporate this devotion as part of your Advent celebration. You will see the Lamb gives reason for Heaven and Earth to rejoice!

—**Will Wall, Associational Missions Strategist, Pine Belt Baptist Association**

We often lose the wonder of Christmas in presents, meals, and tinsel. *It Took A Lamb* helps break through the noise and distractions to bring you the majesty and glory of the Christmas story. Read these devotions slowly and intently. Find your way back to a manger with a Savior who was born to save His people from their sins. That is good news! I'm thankful for the authors' effort to push us to focus on Christ. Be reminded of who He is and refreshed by what He's done.

—**Brian Sanders, Executive Vice-President, Positive Alternative Radio**

With the hustle and bustle of the Christmas season, every believer could benefit from this amazing book to help refocus on the true meaning of Christmas. The journey from Bethlehem to the cross to the Resurrection is so aptly penned. Thank you, Scott and Ray, for leading us along this Christmas journey.

—**Hal and Pamela Santos, Founders, Minister-to-Minister Outreach**

Through *It Took a Lamb,* Cummings and Hanberry take the reader on an exciting and unique 41-day journey to Christmas. Though we focus on the birth of Jesus at Christmas time, the authors remind us the cross was never very far away. Jesus would indeed be the sacrificial lamb. As John the Baptist said, "Behold! The Lamb of God who takes away the sin of the world" (John 1:29). This would be a great way for churches and individuals to make their way to a more meaningful Christmas season.

—**David Hamilton, Pastor, West Heights Baptist Church, Pontotoc, MS**

In this 41-day Advent devotional by Pastors Scott Hanberry and Ray Cummings, don't miss the chance to journey through Scripture—inspired by the brilliant music of Geron and Becky Davis—and learn how Jesus is the Lamb of God, worthy of blessing and honor, glory and power. What does a lamb have to do with Christmas? As Scott and Ray say, "Everything!"

—**Dr. Benjamin Quinn, Associate Professor of Theology and History of Ideas, Southeastern Baptist Theological Seminary**

IT TOOK A LAMB

A 41-DAY CHRISTMAS JOURNEY

DR. RAY CUMMINGS
DR. SCOTT HANBERRY

THE 41 SERIES

It Took a Lamb

Purpose Announced

Passover Lamb

Prophets Revealed

Personal Shepherd

Perfect Reminder

Pictured in Scripture

Portrayed at Calvary

Protection and Restoration

Promised Victory

Day of Victory

FOREWORD

Christmas! The very word brings smiles, excitement, and fond memories. The thoughts of family, friends, trees, lights, music, and parades flood our minds. For children, the word evokes wishful images of parties, presents, and stockings filled with surprises! Within themselves, these things are beautiful images of one of the world's favorite holidays. We each have a favorite song, food, or fun story we repeat every single year. But what about the real story—the true beginning, the real meaning of Christmas? Do our children truly know what the celebration is really all about?

Of course, we all know the elements of the traditional Nativity—a manger, a baby, a star. We are familiar with angels, Mary and Joseph, wise men, and shepherds. We possibly have those beautifully carved pieces on the mantle, table, or piano. The real story of Christmas, however, started long before Bethlehem. In fact, before the foundation of the world, there was a plan for the redemption of the world in a perfect, spotless Lamb.

In this incredible new book, *It Took A Lamb*, my friends Dr. Scott Hanberry and Dr. Ray Cummings walk us through each step of the Advent celebration. With all my heart, I believe it will change your perspective of Christmas. I encourage you to walk through it with your loved ones. Start a new holiday tradition with this book. Share the story, hear the message, and gain a renewed sense of the hope given to all the world in a tiny baby boy. Jesus. King of Kings? Yes. Lord of all? Absolutely. But truly grasp the knowledge that He did not come to earth with that accompanying splendor.

Why did Jesus decide to enter the world the way He did? Certainly He could have been a tad more royal in His entrance. I mean, after all, He was the King of Kings. But He didn't come on a white horse or with the fanfare of a military band heralding His entrance. He didn't arrive in a palace, or a cathedral, but instead chose a manger as His doorway to humanity. Why? Because He knew... it took a Lamb.

Geron Davis
Songwriter/Worship Leader

INTRODUCTION

As I write this introduction for *It Took a Lamb*, my three children are on the verge of flying away from the nest my wife and I started building over thirty years ago. My daughter is a cosmetologist who would have been gone two years ago if the housing market where I live had not gone bonkers. My older son is less than a year from earning the first doctorate in family history; he is living with us for another season as he works through his physical therapy clinicals. My younger son is in his second year of college and figuring things out as he progresses toward a degree.

Even as our children count down to their individual launches into adulthood and fulfill their purposes in this life, my wife and I can't disconnect them from five years ago, ten years ago, fifteen years ago, twenty years ago.... You get the picture. The older two grew up with each other as their most constant companions while my youngest roamed our subdivision streets and surrounding fields with his neighborhood companions. Though their experiences were different, Loretta and I can seen how they shaped each child.

Sometimes, Loretta and I still recall the births of our three children, each unique in their own right. Our daughter was born less than a year after we lost our first child to miscarriage. A few months into Loretta's pregnancy with Ashton, we thought we had lost her, too, but she was born with no complications a few days shy of her October 31 due date. The slightly early delivery was probably beneficial for her since I had already offered a handful of Halloween-related nicknames to pin on her. Garrett was a preemie who had to stay in the hospital for a couple of weeks for extra attention before we could bring him home. Drew was born healthy and on time, but his delivery, shall we say, caused discomfort for my wife that still manifests itself with fidgeting in the passenger seat on long car trips two decades later.

You're welcome for the extended recollection of my children's lives. It has a purpose. As you read the devotionals on this journey, you will likely find yourself wondering if this Christmas devotional wouldn't be better served as an Easter devotional. The truth is, just as my wife and I can't separate who our children are now with the events of their childhoods and the circumstances of their births, the Christian wouldn't be able to rejoice over the sacrifice of the Lamb of God without God's sending Jesus to the world in people skin in the first place.

I communicated often with Ray and Scott as they were working their way through ideas for this Christmas journey with you. I remember how they were particularly struck and inspired by the second verse of the song "It Took a Lamb," written by Geron and Becky Davis, which then instructed the

direction of their writing for the devotional you now hold in
your hands.

> *For many years the temple altars,*
> *Were stained with sacrifices everyday.*
> *And though the blood appeased the Father,*
> *Still the curse of sin was never wiped away.*
> *Till one day the Rule of Justice was halted*
> *By a touch from Mercy's Hand.*
> *Compassion said it's time,*
> *To send the Spotless Lamb.*[1]

Notice the words "...it's time to send the Spotless Lamb."
This was the Lamb slain from the foundation of the world,
God's plan to redeem fallen man. Jesus' sacrifice on the cross,
coupled with His resurrection, is the ultimate event in human
history. If you were to bring the best and brightest minds
throughout history into a room to come up with the best way
for God to bridge the sin gap between Himself and fallen
man, that group of scholars would have never considered
this. God, though, whose thoughts and ways are higher than
even the best minds humankind can offer, so loved the world
that He sent His only Son as a sacrificial Lamb for all people
from all places throughout all time. But the first step in God's
redemptive plan was for Jesus to be born. Before the cross
and the empty tomb, there was the manger.

As my wife and I look back on the lives of our children,
we can put together the pieces of why they have turned out
like they have... so far. Our goal is for you to experience the
same during this Christmas journey. As you read each day's
reflections on the Lamb of God from a perspective of a fuller
picture of the mission Jesus fulfilled, let your mind go back to

the wonder of the manger when angels announced the arrival of God in the flesh. And if you can't separate the words on the page from the Easter story, that's okay; it is all part of the same miraculous story of God's redemption. God's plan came to fulfillment when He sacrificed His son for us. For you. But first, to set His plan into motion in human time, God sent Jesus to earth. Especially since we know the Easter part of the story, Christmas is a time to look forward and celebrate!

Al Ainsworth
Author/Speaker/Teacher

DAY 1

A Look at the Lamb

The next day John saw Jesus coming toward him and said,
"Look! The Lamb of God who takes away the sin of the
world!"
John 1:29

The following day John was again standing with two of his
disciples. As Jesus walked by, John looked at Him and
declared, "Look! There is the Lamb of God!" When John's
two disciples heard this, they followed Jesus.
John 1:35-37

*"Faith is not a once-done act, but a continuous gaze of the heart at
the Triune God. Believing, then, is directing the hearts' attention to
Jesus. It is lifting the mind to 'behold the Lamb of God,' and never
ceasing that beholding for the rest of our lives."*
A.W. Tozer[1]

WHEN JOHN the Baptist announced the Messiah's arrival, he referred to Jesus as the Lamb of God. Two days in a row, John heralded Jesus as the Lamb. Why would John describe Jesus as the Lamb? Because it would take a perfect sacrifice to take away the sin of the world. Only the Lamb would qualify. Israel was all too familiar with the sacrificial system and the Old Testament requirement for a spotless lamb. In the days ahead, we will discuss the Passover Lamb and journey through the topic of the Lamb revealed by the prophets. We will consider our personal Shepherd and the Lamb pictured in Scripture and portrayed at Calvary. We will culminate our journey with the promised victory of the Lamb of God, Who is worthy of our praise, in heaven, . By the time we conclude this journey, we will have sufficient proof that for your salvation and mine, it took a Lamb.

It is intriguing that the title of *Lamb* is the term most often used to describe Jesus in all of Scripture. In fact, Jesus is called the Lamb 104 times in God's Word. Over twenty-five percent of those occurrences are found in the last book of the Bible, the book of Revelation. Repeatedly in heaven, when people see Jesus on His throne, they say, "Worthy is the Lamb." Forever in heaven, our worship of Jesus will be connected to His sacrifice for our sins, His taking our place on the cross. Nothing is more important than beholding the Lamb of God, who takes away the sins of the world.

Celebrating Christmas requires mentioning Jesus' sacrifice. Consider the meaning of Christmas, named after a Holy Day. The Christmas Day 2019 edition of *Newsweek* magazine, shares the following research on the name for Christmas:

Initially, Jesus' birth celebration was called the Feast of the Nativity and was celebrated in England by the end of the sixth century, according to History.com. The first known use of Christmas, according to Merriam-Webster, was before the 12th century and originates from Middle English's *Christemass*, meaning "Christ's mass." Encyclopedia Britannica explained that the term "Christmas" is of "fairly recent origin," and Dictionary.com reported the Christ part of the word Christmas derived from the Greek word Chrīstos, spelled Χριστός in Greek.[2]

Mass became a common term to describe the celebration of the Lord's Supper. So *Christmas* comes from the word *Christ* as our Messiah and *mass*, the celebration of His sacrifice for us on the cross. Every time we say *Merry Christmas*, we are actually remembering His sacrificial death as we celebrate His birth. Jesus came to die as the sacrificial Lamb. We will spend this season of *41 Days* focusing on the Lamb in Scripture because Jesus was born to die. As a follower of Jesus Christ, one cannot celebrate His birth without concentrating on the purpose for which He came. That purpose was to become the sacrificial death for the payment of our sins. He did this as God's Passover Lamb.

Galatians 4:4 reads, "But when the set time had fully come, God sent His Son, born of a woman, born under the law, to redeem those under the law, that we might receive adoption to sonship." In other words, when the time was right, God sent His Lamb into the world. Thirty-three years later, at the time to sacrifice lambs for the Passover, the Father sent His Son to the cross as the ultimate sacrifice for our sins.

Thank you for taking this journey with us this Christmas. As we follow the symbol of the lamb through Scripture, we hope you will draw closer to Jesus, the Lamb of God. May we remember daily that only the Lamb of God can take away the sin of the world. This Christmas, and every Christmas, may we remember His sacrifice. May every Lord's Supper remind us of the Lamb who was slain. By discovering Jesus as the Last Lamb and the ultimate sacrifice, may your love for Christ grow deeper and your commitment to Him grow stronger. Behold the Lamb of God! Look at the Lamb!

REFLECT: Revelation 13:8 (NIV) says, "All inhabitants of the earth will worship the beast—all whose names have not been written in the Lamb's book of life, the Lamb who was slain from the creation of the world." Spend time today reflecting on the Lamb of God who was slaughtered for your sins. Meditate on how much God loves you and what it means that Jesus "was slaughtered before the world was made."[3]

RESPOND: As you respond to God this week, take time to thank Jesus that He was and is the sacrificial Lamb, who takes away the sins of the world. May the words to the first verse of "It Took a Lamb" by Geron and Becky Davis inspire your worship of Jesus, the Lamb of God.

> *He could've come in all His splendor,*
> *Greater than the eye has ever seen.*
> *He could've come in robes of scarlet,*
> *And all the world would see that He is King.*
> *He could've ridden on a white horse*
> *As a warrior and conquered every land.*
> *But He knew that if redemption's price were paid,*
> *It would take a Lamb.*[4]

DAY 2

The Spotless Lamb

The animals you choose must be year-old males without
defect, and you may take them from the sheep or the goats.
Exodus 12:5

(You were redeemed) . . . with the precious blood of Christ,
a Lamb without blemish or defect.
1 Peter 1:18-19

*"One of the most interesting points of the Scriptures is their
constant tendency to display Christ; and perhaps one of the most
beautiful figures under which Jesus Christ is ever exhibited in
sacred writ, is the Passover Paschal Lamb."*
C.H. Spurgeon[1]

THE PASSOVER CELEBRATION for the Jew would later become the Lord's Supper for the Christian. The Passover stems from that final plague that God sent to warn Pharaoh to let His people go. Exodus 11 records the tenth plague, the killing of all firstborn sons in Egypt. Every Hebrew family would be safe if they followed the commands of the Lord. God gave them detailed instructions on how to sacrifice the blood of a spotless lamb in Exodus 12:7: "… they are to take some of the blood and put it on the sides and tops of the doorframes of the houses where they eat the lambs." In Exodus 12:13, God declared, "The blood will be a sign for you on the houses where you are, and when I see the blood, I will pass over you. No destructive plague will touch you when I strike Egypt." If they handled the blood of the spotless lamb correctly, God would pass over them, and they would be saved. The name *Passover* resulted from this occasion.

Exodus 12 reveals the requirements for the Passover lamb. We will look more closely at the Lamb of God as we walk through this Scripture over the next six days. Each day, we will unveil a new comparison from the Passover lambs in Exodus to Jesus, our eternal Passover Lamb.

The phrase *without defect* means "to be perfect or complete." Philip Ryken, in his commentary on Exodus, explains that the lamb for Passover had to be spotless:

Each household was to choose its own lamb, specifically a yearling. It had to be perfect. The lamb was destined to serve as a sacrifice for sin, and the only sacrifice acceptable to God is a perfect sacrifice; so the lamb had to be pure and spotless, whole and sound…. Because God is holy, the only sacrifice that pleases Him is the very best we have to offer.[2]

The reason the lamb had to be "without blemish" or "spotless" was two-fold. Foremost, the Passover lamb was a picture and foreshadowing of Jesus Christ, the Lamb of God. Scripture declares repeatedly that Jesus was the sinless Son of God (See 1 Peter 2:22, 2 Corinthians 5:21, Hebrews 4:15, and 1 John 3:5). Christ is the only One who ever lived a perfect life. He had to be sinless because only a perfect sacrifice would atone for the sins of the world. The shedding of blood from the Spotless Lamb, with blood untainted by the stain of sin, was indispensable for redemption that could satisfy the legal requirement in the court of heaven. Jesus was the righteous dying for the unrighteous, the innocent dying for the guilty, the sinless dying for the sinner. If His life had one blemish, He could not be the Savior of the world.

The second reason the lamb was spotless is God's standard of holiness. God's superiority deserves the best offering. God wants the finest and our best. Why would you bring your worst lamb to sacrifice in worship to the Lord? What love does it display to God if a shepherd brought him a three-legged lamb that he was already going to kill? When we bring God our best, it shows our level of love and allegiance to Him. Exodus 12:5 also gives specific instructions that the animal must be a one-year-old. A one-year-old lamb would require a year of hard work and investment by the shepherd. The shepherd would have to feed it, care for it, and raise it. It would cost the shepherd resources and time. God deserves our best sacrifice. He merits a sacrifice of highest praise.

REFLECT: Since we will look at Exodus 12 for the next several days, it would be beneficial for you to read all fifty-one verses of this great chapter in one sitting. As you read, envision the lamb of the first Passover and meditate on the correlation to Jesus as your Passover Lamb.

RESPOND: As you respond to God this week, praise Him for His sinless life, His sacrificial death, your redemption, and His resurrection. May 1 Peter 1:18-19 be a prompting for your praise.

DAY 3

The Slaughtered Lamb

Take care of them until the fourteenth day of the month,
when all the people of the community of Israel must
slaughter them at twilight.
Exodus 12:6

But He was pierced for our transgressions,
He was crushed for our iniquities;
the punishment that brought us peace was upon Him,
and by His wounds we are healed.
Isaiah 53:5

*"The Christian icon is not the Stars and Stripes, but a cross-flag,
and it's emblem is not a donkey, an elephant, or an eagle,
but a slaughtered lamb."*
Shane Claiborne[1]

9

THE PASSOVER IS a major portrait in the hallway of our faith. In addition, lambs were a focal point in biblical worship throughout Scripture. A magnificent scene in appears in 1 Kings 8:62-63 during the dedication of Solomon's temple:

> Then the king and all of Israel with him offered sacrifices before the Lord. Solomon offered a sacrifice of fellowship offerings to the Lord: twenty-two thousand cattle and a hundred and twenty thousand sheep and goats. So the king and all the Israelites dedicated the temple of the Lord.

This would have been an unbelievable sight and sacrifice. Can you imagine what it would take to butcher 142,000 animals and offer them in a worship service? The size of this slaughter was gigantic and gruesome. Not only would it require a great deal of time, but it would also reveal an enormous amount of trust. To offer that many animals, Israel would need a great faith that the Lord could provide the future food they would need to feed their nation.

Exodus 12:6 specifically uses the word *slaughter*. We often think of Jesus as our sacrifice without considering the implication that Christ was slaughtered. Sacrifice sounds so much easier to say, but the fact is that Jesus was slaughtered to save us from our sins. Isaiah prophetically saw the cross 700 years before it happened and wrote the gruesome details of what would happen to Jesus at Calvary. Isaiah 53:5 states that Jesus was pierced, crushed, punished, and wounded.

Without understanding the details of His slaughtering sacrifice, we will not fully understand the depth of His love. God so loved the world that He picked the worst time in history to send His Son to die for our sins. If God sent His son in our generation, the worst thing that would happen to the

Lamb of God would have been lethal injection. Yet God chose a place and time in all of all humankind's existence, a segment in history where capital punishment would include the brutality of crucifixion. In that specific time, God sent Jesus to the slaughter of the cross to be the ultimate sacrifice for our sins. With that thought in mind, Romans 5:8 has more impact on our thoughts. "But God demonstrated His own love for us in this: While we were still sinners, Christ died for us."

In south Mississippi, sometimes I will pass a truck full of cattle headed to the slaughterhouse. Other times, I will pass a big rig full of chickens headed to be processed. I can't help but think that those animals have no idea where they are headed. The day will not end well for them, and they are completely clueless that their demise is coming soon.

This is one area where the Passover lamb analogy with Jesus breaks down. While Passover lambs are a great comparison and illustration of Jesus, the Lamb of God, this is one area where Jesus differs from the sacrificial lambs. We will deal with this idea in detail on Day 11, but I would like to just mention it today. The Passover lambs didn't know they were headed to slaughter. Jesus knew He was destined to die and still willingly gave His life for our sins.

REFLECT: Reflect on the cruelty of the cross and the slaughtering of our Passover Lamb. As you meditate on His sacrifice, write down your thoughts on how much God loves you.

RESPOND: As Christmas approaches, keep your focus on your Lord who came as a Lamb, your Savior who was slaughtered. Perhaps your focus on His sacrifice will strengthen your resolve to daily surrender your will to His.

DAY 4

The Shared Lamb

If any household is too small for a whole lamb,
they must share one with their nearest neighbor.
Exodus 12:4

God was reconciling the world to Himself in Christ, not
counting men's sins against them. And He has committed to
us the message of reconciliation.
2 Corinthians 5:19

"The gospel is good news only if it arrives in time."
Carl F. H. Henry [1]

GOD WAS specific in His commands concerning the way the Lamb was to be prepared. Exodus 12:9-11 clarifies the process:

> Do not eat the meat raw or boiled in water, but roast it over a fire—with the head, legs and internal organs. Do not leave any of it till morning; if some is left till morning, you must burn it. This is how you are to eat it: with your cloak tucked into your belt, your sandals on your feet and your staff in your hand. Eat it in haste; it is the Lord's Passover.

Thus, the lamb had to be roasted and completely consumed. Any part that was not eaten had to be burned. The Hebrews had to eat the lamb with urgency, as symbolized by eating with their sandals on, staff in hand, and cloak tucked in. They had to be ready to go because this was serious business. Life and death were hanging in the balance.

It is extremely interesting to me that Exodus 12:4 says that the Passover lamb was shared. You couldn't have leftover lamb. Since it all had to be consumed, it needed to be shared. Most lambs were so large that one household could never eat it all. I have read where one lamb could feed approximately forty people. Therefore, most households were too small to have the lamb just to themselves.

These details would be a future picture for all His children and the household of God. God wants the Lamb to be shared. We must invite people to partake of the Lamb of God.

At times, people will say about a certain church: "That church is just too big." In actuality, all churches are too small, because there is more Lamb to be served. No matter how many people are saved and are growing in their faith, there is always more Lamb to be shared. The Lamb of God is sufficient for the entire world to consume and be saved. When Jesus comes back for His church, He doesn't want leftover Lamb. He sent His Son, the Lamb of God, so that all people could have the opportunity to be saved by His sacrifice.

We should share the Lamb today with the same urgency that the Hebrews shared their lambs at Passover time. Life is too short, and death is all too sure for us to be apathetic and lethargic when it comes to sharing our faith.

Mark Cahill, a former Auburn basketball player turned soul winner, wrote a book entitled *One Thing You Can't Do in Heaven*. The premise of the book is since there won't be any evangelism or soul-winning in heaven, we need to be doing it now. I love Cahill's passion and urgency for reaching the lost: "The only time we lose is when we don't share our faith. Every other time it is a winning situation."[2] Cahill is correct —we can never go wrong by sharing our faith.

Exodus 12:11 ends with these words, "... Eat it in haste; it is the Lord's Passover." The word *Passover* in the Hebrew language is *pesa*. It is repeated later in verse 13, "… I will pass over you." The primary meaning of this word is God's passing over the houses with the blood of the lamb. However, this Hebrew word also means "to have compassion" and "to protect." If the Israelites obeyed God's commands, God would have compassion for His children and protect them from harm. Likewise, God wants to protect the world from the penalty and punishment of sin. That's why God sent His Son as a Lamb. God is a compassionate and gracious God. Thus, He gave us the command to be fishers of men, ordered us to make disciples, and gave us the ministry of reconciliation.

Let's go share the Lamb so that the lost can receive the gift of salvation through Jesus Christ!

REFLECT: Consider seriously with urgency what God's Word says in 2 Corinthians 5:19: "… He has committed to us the message of reconciliation."

RESPOND: Another quote from Mark Cahill's book is "Jesus did His part two thousand years ago, and now it is time for you to do yours."[3] How will you respond to His calling on your life this week? Go share the Lamb.

DAY 5

T he Substitute Lamb

"On that same night I will pass through Egypt and strike
down every firstborn of both people and animals,
and I will bring judgment on all the gods of Egypt.
I am the Lord. The blood will be a sign for you
on the houses where you are, and when I see the blood,
I will pass over you. No destructive plague will touch you
when I strike Egypt."
Exodus 12:12-13

"The importance of the lamb as a substitute
would not have been lost on the firstborn son.
Once the lamb was chosen, it was kept in the house for four days,
during which time the family fed it, cared for it, and played with it.
In that short time they would have identified with the lamb,
so that it almost became part of the family.

'This is our Passover lamb,' they would say.
Then it was slaughtered, which was a messy, bloody business.
The head of the household took the lamb in his arms,
pulled back its head, and slit its throat.
Red blood spurted all over the lamb's pure white wool.
'Why, Daddy?' the children would say.
Their father would explain that the lamb was a substitute.
The firstborn did not have to die
because the lamb had died in his place."
Philip Ryken and R. Kent Hughes[1]

JESUS SUBSTITUTED Himself for us and took our place at the cross. The sinless Lamb of God died in the place of sinners. At the cross, Jesus took our shame and our blame. Isaiah prophesied in Isaiah 53:6, "We all, like sheep, have gone astray, each of us has turned to our own way; and the LORD has laid on him the iniquity of us all."

One commentary on Isaiah explains the Lord's substitutionary and sacrificial death:

Theologians call this *imputation*, from the Latin verb *imputare*, "to charge (to someone's account)." Guilt must be paid for. It can't be swept under the rug. You know that from your own experience. When you are wronged or injured—even in a fender-bender—someone has to answer for it, either you or the other person. The damage and cost don't just go away. If it's going to be put right, someone has to pay the cost. And so it is with God. There is no way He can turn a blind eye to our evil that is damaging His universe. How did God confront it? How was the damage paid for? Out of love for us, God charged that infinite debt to a substitute. Jesus Christ put Himself in the place of sinners, the unbearable weight of their guilt was imputed to Him, and He sank under it. "God made Him who had no sin to be sin for us, so that in him we might become the righteousness of God" (2 Corinthians 5:21). This is the love of God. Substitution is the very meaning of love.[2]

Our Lord and Lamb of God loved us so much He willingly took our place. Jesus shed His blood to pay our sin debt. Christ sacrificed His life so that our lives could be saved. He took our place on the cross so that we could one day find our place in heaven. Substitution resulted from His love, and the payment was signed in His blood. A commentary on Exodus enlightens us to this truth:

The sign that we have a substitute is the blood of Christ. When we look up to the cross, we see that payment has been made for our sin. And what does God see when He looks down at the cross? He sees it is stained with the blood of His very own firstborn Son. God does not have a substitute to offer in place of His Son; His Son *is* the Substitute! And when God sees the blood of His Son, he says, "It is enough. My justice has been satisfied. The price for sin is fully paid. Death will pass over you, and you will be safe forever.[3]

REFLECT and RESPOND: Reflect on 2 Corinthians 5:21: "God made Him who had no sin to be sin for us, so that in Him we might become the righteousness of God." The Message paraphrases it this way: "In Christ, God put the wrong on Him who never did anything wrong, so we could be put right with God." Because Jesus took your place, you can trade your shameless guilt for His saving grace.

DAY 6

The Symbolic Lamb

"This is how you are to eat it: with your cloak tucked into your belt, your sandals on your feet and your staff in your hand. Eat it in haste; it is the Lord's Passover. . ."
"This is a day you are to commemorate; for the generations to come you shall celebrate it as a festival to the Lord—a lasting ordinance."
Exodus 12:11, 14

"It must be eaten inside the house; take none of the meat outside the house. Do not break any of the bones.
The whole community of Israel must celebrate it.
Exodus 12:46-47

"The Passover is the sign of a greater act of redemption."
Tim Chester[1]

JONATHAN EDWARDS WROTE, "Christ and His redemption are the subject of the whole Word of God."[2] Since the entire Word of God points to His salvation paid for at Calvary, there are numerous scriptural signs that point us to Christ's sacrifice. The first Passover points us to the cross and to Christ. The Passover lamb was symbolically spotless, slaughtered, and shared as a substitute.

Passover lambs sacrificed after the first Passover pointed to Jesus. Experts estimate the time of the first Passover around 1513 BC. Most scholars place the year of Jesus' death around AD 33. For over 1500 years, an entire nation had celebrated Passover. Millions of people over those years remembered the Passover. Consider for a moment how many lambs were sacrificed during that timeframe. Every single one of those lambs symbolized Jesus' once-for-all sacrifice. In addition, every one of those millions upon millions of celebrations and remembrances pointed to the cross of Christ and His redemption. Christ is the final sacrifice. He is the Last Lamb. All other lambs are signs pointing to the truth of who Jesus is: the Lamb of God.

The consistent message of the Bible is that anyone who wants to meet God must come based on the Lamb He has provided. All the other lambs prepared for the coming of Christ. A theologian would call them *types*, or signs pointing to salvation in Christ. To be sure we don't miss the connection, the New Testament says that "Christ, our Passover lamb, has been sacrificed" (1 Corinthians 5:7b).[3]

God made sure no one could miss the significance of the Passover as a symbol pointing to Jesus' sacrifice by perfectly timing Jesus' death on the cross. Scripture continually emphasizes this truth. John 13:1 reads, "It was just before the Passover Festival. Jesus knew that the hour had come for

Him to leave this world and go to the Father...." John 18:28 emphasizes this truth when Jesus stood on trial before Pilate: "Then the Jewish leaders took Jesus from Caiaphas to the palace of the Roman governor. By now it was early morning, and to avoid ceremonial uncleanness they did not enter the palace, because they wanted to be able to eat the Passover."

The day Jesus made His triumphal entry into Jerusalem was the very day that the Passover lambs were driven into the city, and when Jesus celebrated the Last Supper with His disciples, He was celebrating the Passover (Matthew 26:17). He said, "This is my body... This is my blood" (vs. 26–28). His disciples didn't understand it at the time, but Jesus was really saying, "The Passover is all about Me. I am the sacrificial lamb."

Then Christ was crucified. It was late in the afternoon on the eve of Passover. At twilight, lambs would be sacrificed by every household, according to the Law of Moses. All over the city, fathers were getting ready to make the offering, gathering their families together and saying, "God has provided a lamb for us." Over at the temple, the high priest was also preparing a lamb to present as an atonement for Israel's sin. Then there was Jesus, hanging on the cross, with the sacrificial blood flowing from His hands and side. He was the Lamb of God taking away the sins of the world.[4]

REFLECT and RESPOND: Spend some time in prayer reflecting on the timing of Jesus' sacrifice. Take some time in worship to personally celebrate over the millions of past celebrations that have all pointed to Jesus. He is the Lamb, worthy of all our praise!

DAY 7

The Saving Lamb

Get rid of the old yeast, so that you may be a new unleavened
batch as you really are. For Christ, our Passover lamb, has
been sacrificed. Therefore let us keep the Festival, not with
the old bread leavened with malice and wickedness, but with
the unleavened bread of sincerity and truth.
1 Corinthians 5:7-8

"Either sin is with you, lying on your shoulders,
or it is lying on Christ, the Lamb of God.
Now if it is lying on our back, you are lost;
but if it is resting on Christ, you are free, and you will be saved.
Now choose what you want."
Martin Luther[1]

THOSE WHO REGULARLY CELEBRATE Passover can better relate to what Paul was sharing with the church at Corinth in 1 Corinthians 5:7. The Jews have kept this tradition for over 3000 years. In the first Passover, recorded in Exodus 12, the people had to hurry because they were getting ready to flee Pharaoh. Therefore, the first participants in Passover made their bread without leaven so that they could cook it hurriedly, carry it more easily, and eat it quickly. That is why God gave them explicit orders regarding the celebration in Exodus 12:14-16:

> This is a day you are to commemorate; for the generations to come you shall celebrate it as a festival to the Lord—a lasting ordinance. For seven days you are to eat bread made without yeast. On the first day remove the yeast from your houses, for whoever eats anything with yeast in it from the first day through the seventh must be cut off from Israel. On the first day hold a sacred assembly, and another one on the seventh day. Do no work at all on these days, except to prepare food for everyone to eat; that is all you may do.

While bread without yeast had a practical everyday purpose, yeast—or leaven—also had a spiritual significance. Tom Wright makes this connection in his writings on 1 Corinthians:

> In Paul's world, when people spoke of leaven in a metaphorical sense, it was almost always a way of talking about a bad influence corrupting something that would otherwise be pure.... (Paul) is pulling out a Passover-image because at the center of Christianity is a Passover-event, indeed *the* Passover-event. From the very beginning, the

early church believed that it hadn't just been a coincidence that Jesus died (and rose again) at Passover-time; this was how God wanted it. The timing explained the meaning.

At the first Passover, each family slaughtered a lamb for their evening meal, and put its blood on the doorposts of the house so that the angel of death would 'pass over' them and spare them, while the firstborn of the Egyptians were killed. When Jews of Paul's day kept the Passover festival, they sacrificed lambs in the Temple, continuing the tradition and keeping fresh the memory of God's great deliverance. The early Christians saw Jesus' own death as the climax, the culmination, of this whole tradition. He was the real Passover lamb, and His death had won deliverance for the whole world.

The whole Christian life, from this point of view, becomes one long Passover-celebration![2]

Yeast is a symbol of sin. Sin is so serious that Jesus died to provide our forgiveness. Jesus lived a perfect life and died a sacrificial death for one purpose: to provide salvation for your soul. The first Passover lambs saved the Jews from the death of their first-born sons. The sacrifice of Jesus as our Passover Lamb saves every single person who chooses to put his or her faith in Christ. The wages of sin is death, but the sacrifice of Jesus leads to eternal life. That's why the Bible refers to salvation as being born again because the Lamb saves.

Because the Lamb is our Lord, our lives should consist worship of remembrance and celebration to the Lamb who saves. The Lamb's sacrifice allows every believer to live as "a new unleavened batch as you really are."

REFLECT: Consider what Paul meant by 1 Corinthians 5:7: "Get rid of the old yeast, so that you may be a new unleavened batch as you really are. For Christ, our Passover lamb, has been sacrificed."

RESPOND: Allow what Paul shared in 1 Corinthians 5:8 to challenge your response: "Therefore let us keep the Festival, not with the old bread leavened with malice and wickedness, but with the unleavened bread of sincerity and truth."

DAY 8

A **Prophetic Picture of Peace**

"In that day the wolf and the lamb will live together; the
leopard will lie down with the baby goat. The calf and the
yearling will be safe with the lion,
and a little child will lead them all."
Isaiah 11:6

"The wolf and the lamb will feed together. The lion will eat
hay like a cow. But the snakes will eat dust. In those days no
one will be hurt or destroyed on my holy mountain.
I, the Lord, have spoken!"
Isaiah 65:25

"After a hard day scrambling to find your way around in the world, it's assuring to come home to a place you know. God can be equally familiar to you. With time you can learn where to go for nourishment, where to hide for protection, where to turn for guidance. Just as your earthly house is a place of refuge, so God's house is a place of peace."
Max Lucado[1]

OVER THE NEXT FOUR DAYS, we will look at what the prophets revealed about the Lamb. Each prophecy sheds light on the Lamb of God, who takes away the sin of the world. As we look at the Lamb, we find comfort, unconditional love, and spiritual transformation. As we look at the prophecies concerning a lamb, we find clarity, insight, and inspiration.

As we move toward the celebration of Jesus' birth, we also celebrate His life, death, and resurrection. Remember, the title *Christmas* represents Christ and the Lord's Supper, the mass. As Jesus came to die, we cannot celebrate His birth without commemorating His death. Jesus was born to die, and we can't really live spiritually until we die to self and surrender our will to His. If applicable, may your celebration of Jesus' birthday lead to you being born again. If you are already a Christ-follower, may His birthday party provide inspiration to birth in you a closer walk with Him.

Isaiah prophecies two interesting statements about the wolf and the lamb. In Isaiah 11, the prophet foretells about a day when "the wolf and lamb will live together." In Isaiah 65, he forecasts a day when "the wolf and lamb will feed together." A wolf is the natural and known predator of the lamb. Lambs have every right to fear the wolf because it is the nature of the wolf to want to devour the lamb. Therefore,

Isaiah speaks of a day when there will finally be peace between these two adversaries.

When will this day take place? Many scholars believe Isaiah is referring to the time when Christ will return and create a new heaven and a new Earth. John is given a revelation of this through a vision and records this time in Revelation 21:4. One day soon, there will be no more wickedness, wars, pain, or problems. There will be no more crying, frustration, temptation, or desperation. One day, we will live in the presence of the Prince of Peace and will experience forever perfect peace. The lamb and the wolf give us a prophetic picture of peace.

I am looking forward to that day when Jesus returns to replace our pain with peace. Until that day comes, I will practice casting all my anxiety on Him. 1 Peter 5:7 declares, "Cast all your anxiety on Him because He cares for you." The term *anxiety* comes from a New Testament word that means "to separate from the whole or to divide." Anxiety will distract and detour you away from the wholeness that God desires for your life. Anxiety will tear you apart at the seams. This word is the same word found in Philippians 4:6 where Paul says, "Do not be anxious about anything...." The Living Bible paraphrases Philippians 4:6 this way: "Don't worry about anything; instead pray about everything; tell God your needs, and don't forget to thank Him for His answers." This paraphrase goes on to say in verse 7: "If you do this, you will experience God's peace, which is far more wonderful than the human mind can understand. His peace will keep your hearts quiet and at rest as you trust in Christ Jesus." The word *peace* is a Greek word that means "to join or tie together into a whole." While anxiety divides you, the peace of God brings everything in your life back together. Worry detaches; peace connects. Worry separates; peace unites. The peace of God makes you whole.

REFLECT: Read Revelation 21:1-4. As you read, consider deeply the time when God will make a new heaven and a new earth for all of His children. As you contemplate this beautiful picture, envision the wolf and lamb living together and feeding together.

RESPOND: Are there places in your life that are filled with anxiety? What is dividing your spirit and pulling you apart? Pray for the peace of God that passes all understanding to guard your hearts and minds in Christ Jesus. Respond today by praying Philippians 4:7 over your life.

DAY 9

A Prophetic Picture of Protection

See, the Sovereign Lord comes with power, and He rules
with a mighty arm. See, His reward is with Him,
and His recompense accompanies Him.
He will feed His flock like a shepherd.
He will carry the lambs in His arms,
holding them close to His heart.
He will gently lead the mother sheep with their young.
Isaiah 40:10-11

*"A God wise enough to create me and the world I live in
is wise enough to watch out for me."*
Philip Yancey [1]

Isaiah 40 speaks to the people of God who are exiled and imprisoned. This Scripture speaks to a nation that has become disheartened, disillusioned, and depressed. In their confused state, they are prone to think that God has somehow failed them. Through the power of God's Spirit, Isaiah saw beyond his own day and the nation's impending captivity and spoke into a future context of a coming Messiah. Isaiah is telling them that soon they would find themselves in Babylonian exile. When that happened, they would think God had abandoned them. This prophet of God is telling them, when that day happens, don't lose sight of Who is protecting you. God would not desert them, nor would He forsake them. God would come to save His people. When they found themselves in their predicted future, he warned them to not forget the protection of their God. The Messiah was coming for them. The first Christmas for them was in their future. Their hope was in the protection of their Great Deliverer who would come to set the captives free.

Wouldn't it give you great hope to be told ahead of time to remember God's provisions and protection? It would strengthen all people if we approached our daily lives from the viewpoint and perspective that we have a Heavenly Father who defends, shields, shelters, and safeguards His children. If we wait until trouble comes, we might not have the wherewithal to live from the proper biblical outlook that God cares for and secures His own. Before every storm of life arrives, we need to be reminded that we have a God who delivers and saves.

Notice the terminology Isaiah uses in his words of wisdom and warning. Verse 10 states that "the Sovereign Lord comes with power" and "rules with a mighty arm." God comes with a "powerful hand." The Lord also comes with a "reward" and "recompense." The King James Version translates this text "His reward is with Him and His work before Him." This powerful hand of God is holding a prize for His people who are faithful to His work. Not only does He protect with His power, but He also provides. The same hand that rules is the same hand that rewards.

Isaiah 40:11 continues this picture of protection by stating that "He will feed His flock like a Shepherd." One of the shepherd's responsibilities was to lead his sheep to green pastures. When that pasture had been eaten down by the sheep, the shepherd was responsible for leading them to another pasture to continue to provide food for them. As the Great Shepherd, the Lord always provides leadership for the continual feeding of His sheep. The Lord guides and provides.

Scripture continues by stating, "He will carry the lambs in His arms, holding them close to His heart. He will gently lead the mother sheep with their young."[2] Our Lord carries and embraces. The fact that our Shepherd carries His lambs in His arms depicts lovingkindness. The detailed description that He holds us close to His heart signifies His care and compassion. With the same hand that holds, He helps. Isaiah's picture of protection is a beautiful depiction of the love of our Lord.

God's love is both personal and protective. He works in our lives with a powerful hand that rules but also with a tender arm that relates. His authority is superior, yet His approach is sensitive. The Lamb of God is a powerful yet personal provider and protector. No matter our circumstances, He has the might and means to minister to His sheep. We can find comfort in that.

REFLECT: Spend some time today thinking about how much your Shepherd loves and cares for you. The beginning of 1 John 3:1 provides a great perspective. "See what great love the Father has lavished on us, that we should be called children of God!"

RESPOND: As you pray and put God's Word into practice in your life, allow the following quote by A.W. Tozer to encourage your worship: "The only safe place for a sheep is by the side of His shepherd, because the devil does not fear sheep; he just fears the Shepherd."[3]

DAY 10

Silent before His Shearers

All of us, like sheep, have strayed away.
We have left God's paths to follow our own.
Yet the Lord laid on Him the sins of us all.
He was oppressed and treated harshly,
yet He never said a word.
He was led like a lamb to the slaughter.
And as a sheep is silent before the shearers,
He did not open His mouth.
Isaiah 53:6-7

*"The possibility of substitution rests on the identity
of the substitute."*
John R.W. Stott[1]

ISAIAH'S PROPHECY in Isaiah 53:6-7 graphically portrays our suffering Savior's sacrifice as the substitute for our sins. Since we discussed "The Lamb as Our Substitute" on Day 5, we will focus more today on Isaiah's prophetic picture of Jesus' patient persistence as He suffered in our place.

Seven hundred years before Jesus died on the cross at Calvary, Isaiah clearly depicted the analogy between a scapegoat and our Savior and a sheared Lamb to our beaten Lord. The scapegoat is portrayed by the words, "Yet the Lord laid on Him the sins of us all." And the sheared lamb is described by the statement, "And as a sheep is silent before the shearers, He did not open His mouth." In these two comparisons, Isaiah predicted that Jesus would never say a word during his scourging and likened His sacrifice to a lamb led to a slaughter.

The prophetic clarity of Isaiah's writing is amazing, while the picturesque comparison of Jesus to a lamb is enlightening. The scapegoat would symbolically carry the sins of the people away into the wilderness; our Savior would sacrificially carry our sins away forever. Sheep would be sheared for their wool; we will find forgiveness through His wounds. A lamb is so innocent that it is silent while it is being sheared; the Lamb was so blameless that He was silent while He suffered. The Savior didn't speak at all while He was being beaten; His salvation speaks eternally into our lives. He left His throne in heaven and took our place on the cross; we can be forgiven of our sins and find His place in heaven.

Isaiah 53:7 describes what would happen to our scapegoat, the Savior, and to our Lord, the Lamb: He would be oppressed, treated harshly, slaughtered, and sheared. First, He would be oppressed. The original meaning of this word is "to hard press, drive vehemently to work, and to distress."

This word was often used in biblical times to describe how taskmasters miserably mistreated their slaves. Slave owners would often hassle and torment their slaves. The Lamb of God was hounded and harassed by His enemies.

Second, Scripture says that our Lamb was afflicted. The Hebrew Old Testament word means "to be humbled, to be put down, or become low." It means to be humbled by being mistreated. Our Lord and Savior humbled Himself and became obedient unto death, even death on a cross (See Philippians 2:8).

Next, Jesus was "led like a lamb to the slaughter." The term *led* means "to be carried or brought to." The word *slaughter* is a simile of our Suffering Servant. This Old Testament word often referred to the slaughter of animals. It is a frightening experience to know that people are leading you to the slaughter. Jesus was led to His brutal killing like a lamb was led to a butcher.

Finally, Jesus was sheared like a lamb. The Roman soldiers stripped Jesus of His clothes and shamefully and brutally crucified Him before the onlooking crowd. His back was laid bare from the scourging, and He was killed as a public display of brutality.

How did Jesus respond when He was oppressed, treated harshly, sheared, and slaughtered? Silence. "He never said a word. He did not open His mouth." Jesus accepted His Father's will that He would be the substitute for our sins. The Bible clearly states the comparison, "... as a sheep is silent before the shearers..." Sheep are docile and compliant as they submit themselves to their shearer. It is a sign of complete submission. Jesus completely submitted in silence to the will of His Father and gave His life as a ransom for many.

REFLECT: Meditate more on today's quote by theologian John R.W. Stott: "The possibility of substitution rests on the identity of the substitute." What do you think this statement means and why?

RESPOND: As you look to the Lamb and experience Him in your personal walk with Him, contemplate the picture of a sheep before his shearers. Praise Him for His submission and silence, and the ultimate price Christ paid as your substitute.

DAY 11

K nowledge of God's Plan

Because the Lord revealed their plot to me, I knew it,
for at that time He showed me what they were doing.
I was like a lamb being led to the slaughter.
I had no idea that they were planning to kill me!
"Let's destroy this man and all his words," they said.
"Let's cut him down, so his name will be forgotten forever."
Jeremiah 11:18-19

*"All God's plans have the mark of the cross on them,
and all His plans have death to self in them."*
E. M. Bounds[1]

THE PROPHET JEREMIAH was "like a lamb being led to the slaughter." There was a plan to kill Jeremiah and destroy his legacy. He was caught off guard, declaring, "I had no idea that they were planning to kill me." Many prophets, just like Jeremiah, were persecuted without warning.

Like Jeremiah, Jesus was like a lamb being led to the slaughter. Unlike Jeremiah, Jesus knew the Father's plan. Christ saw it coming since the creation of the world. Revelation 13:8 refers to Jesus as the "Lamb slain from the foundation of the world."

Not only did Jesus perceive it, but He also often predicted it. The first time Christ foretold He would die is found in Matthew 16:21-23, Mark 8:31-32, and Luke 9:21-22. Jesus declared His future death a second time in Matthew 17:22-23, Mark 9:30-32, and Luke 9:43-45. A third declaration of His impending death occurs in Matthew 20:17-19, Mark 10:32-34, and Luke 18:31-34. In addition, John's gospel records even more of Jesus' pronouncement of His suffering and death: John 12:7-8, John 13:33, John 14:25, and John 14:29. Scripture is full of proof that Jesus, the Lamb of God, knew the Father's plan.

Jesus knew full well that He was born and sent to this world to die. His death was the foremost purpose of His life and ministry. He knew a perfect sacrifice was required for the remission of sins and that He alone would qualify. One of the amazing facts about Christ's love is that He always knew, yet He still followed through.

As my substitute, Jesus carried the payment for my sins all the way to the cross, the burden of all the sins of the world to the Place of the Skull. Suspended between Earth and heaven, Jesus took my place and lifted up my sin debt to the approval of God. Christ willingly followed through with God's plan for salvation.

When I was a young teenager, I went to a back-to-school retreat at a place in south Mississippi called King's Arrow Ranch. Our church hosted the retreat, and the guest speaker for the weekend was Rhett Whitley. Rhett was an original member of the renowned "Nasty Bunch" defense for the University of Southern Mississippi Golden Eagles' football team. Because of this, he immediately had my attention when he spoke. One morning, he took a huge green duffel bag packed full of items and spoke about carrying the weight of sin. He picked me out of the group and told me to carry it over my shoulder for the rest of the day until that night's devotion. He also said that he better not catch me at any time throughout the day without this bag. So I carried it with me everywhere. I took it to our cabin, to lunch, to recreation time, and even to the bathroom.

About halfway through the day, my identical twin brother, Ricky, came to me and offered to carry it in my place. He said nobody would know the difference, so I gladly handed my burden to him. Ricky saw my dilemma and came to my rescue, so I released that burden for him to carry. I did not realize until later just how vivid a picture God had given me of what His Son, the Lamb of God, had done to willingly take my place and carry the burden of my sin. Ricky took my burden at a place called Kings Arrow; Jesus took my sin debt as my King of kings, and the Lord Almighty. My twin brother chose to take my place; Christ, the friend that sticks closer than a brother, died as my substitute. My earthly brother took my load representing sin and carried it; my Heavenly Father put all my sin on His Son, who bore it at Calvary. Ricky released me of a temporary burden; Jesus carried the eternal weight of my sin and shame. The Lamb of God knew God's plan, and He still carried it to completion.

REFLECT: Think about the love Christ demonstrated on the cross. Read through Matthew's accounts of the predictions of Christ concerning His death: Matthew 16:21-23, Matthew 17:22-23, and Matthew 20:17-19. As you read, direct your attention to His statements and the determination it took for Christ to follow through with the Father's plan.

RESPOND: As you live out God's Word today, keep what E.M Bounds said in the forefront of your minds: "All God's plans have the mark of the cross on them..." Pray, asking God to give you the resolve to take up your cross daily and follow Him.

DAY 12

An Unlikely Audience: Shepherds

That night there were shepherds staying in the fields nearby,
guarding their flocks of sheep. Suddenly, an angel of the Lord
appeared among them, and the radiance of the Lord's glory
surrounded them. They were terrified.
Luke 2:8-9

Instead, God chose things the world considers foolish in
order to shame those who think they are wise. And he chose
things that are powerless to shame those who are powerful.
1 Corinthians 1:27

"If you were a PR agent and you were designing a campaign
to announce that the Savior of the world had been born,
the last people you would go to is a bunch of shepherds."
John MacArthur[1]

ALL THE HOPES and longings and aspirations for a deliverer were about to be fulfilled. The time had come for the Messiah to arrive. Jesus would soon be born. This was not just good news; this was the greatest news ever announced. And that announcement came to an unlikely audience. You might think that information of this magnitude would be delivered to kings, potentates, and dignitaries. At the very least, it seems logical that religious leaders or prophets or priests would be on the short list to receive such grand news first. Yet God had other plans.

According to Luke's gospel, the angelic pronouncement of the birth of the Savior of the world came to shepherds tending their flocks in the middle of the night. This motley group was out in the fields among smelly and dimwitted sheep. These uneducated, simple men had no power, no influence, no clout. General consensus was that shepherds were unreliable, untrustworthy, unsavory characters. They couldn't even testify in court. Shunned as outcasts, shepherds were considered unclean and looked down upon because they were unable to keep the rigorous demands of the law. For example, they worked on the Sabbath (since sheep don't take days off).

Perhaps the reaction of the shepherds gives us a glimpse into why God chose them. They were humbled and amazed. They must have felt quite honored. We read that they were exuberant and quickly went to investigate and then to share. If God had first come to the Pharisees, they might have felt entitled to the news. In their self-righteousness, they might have expected God to come to them. Yet it was these men who watched the sheep meant for the slaughter who received a divine message about the ultimate Lamb, the One who would take away the sins of the world through His death and resurrection.[2]

Consider the words of John MacArthur about the first audience of this angelic announcement:

> Isn't that just like God to disdain the religious elite, to disdain the hypocrites who thought they were good enough to achieve relationships with God by their own self-effort? And to make the greatest announcement that's ever been made in the history of the world to the lowest of the low, the humblest of the humble, shepherds.[3]

God, in His infinite wisdom, chose just the right group of people to entrust the greatest news of eternity. Choosing to reveal Himself to the shepherds demonstrates how He reveals His love to people who were looked down upon and cast out. For that, you and I should be eternally grateful. Walter Wangerin expresses this gratitude:

> "Gloria, Gloria!" they cry, for their song embraces all that the Lord has begun this day: Glory to God in the highest of heavens! And peace to the people with whom he is pleased! And who are these people? With whom does the good Lord choose to take his pleasure? The shepherds. The plain and nameless—whose every name the Lord knows well. You. And me.[4]

Those humble men took the Good News of Jesus and did just what God wanted them to do—told others, and their lives were never the same. They were amazed God chose them, and they couldn't keep it to themselves.

REFLECT: You may feel unworthy, unloveable, or even unlikely that God would be concerned with you. However, today we challenge you to recognize your value in the sight of God. God demonstrated His love for you in the death of His Son, Jesus. You are of infinite worth to Him. In fact, you are worth the premium price tag that it cost Jesus to ransom you from your sins.

RESPOND: Dear Lord, today I rejoice with the shepherds in the Good News of Jesus' birth. Thank you for revealing Your love to me. Help me to experience Your love with awe and amazement. Guide me as I explore the wonder of Jesus' birth and consider the significance of His sacrificial death as the Perfect Lamb. Thank You for sending a Savior for me. I want to spend my life sharing this news. In Jesus' Name, amen.

DAY 13

A n Unbelievable Announcement: Peace

But the angel reassured them. "Don't be afraid!" he said.
"I bring you good news that will bring great joy
to all people. The Savior—yes, the Messiah, the Lord—
has been born today in Bethlehem, the city of David!
And you will recognize him by this sign: You will find a baby
wrapped snugly in strips of cloth, lying in a manger."
Suddenly, the angel was joined by a vast host of others—
the armies of heaven—praising God and saying,
"Glory to God in highest heaven, and peace on earth
to those with whom God is pleased."
Luke 2:10-14

"Then pealed the bells more loud and deep: 'God is not dead, nor doth He sleep; the wrong shall fail, the right prevail, with peace on earth, goodwill to men.'"
Henry Wadsworth Longfellow[1]

Have you ever felt worn down by bad news? I know I have. Days come when I cannot bring myself to turn on the television or scroll through my newsfeed. It seems we are constantly are in the grip of grim headlines. One after another, weighty stories of heartache, tragedy, evil, and pain come. Do you ever feel this weight? It can be downright depressing.

Henry Wadsworth Longfellow found himself in that predicament. A poet in the 1800s, Longfellow faced a personal tragedy that caused him to slide into a pit of depression. His wife had died, and his soul was troubled. A journal entry on Christmas Day in 1862 revealed the despair and grief of his heart. He would record, "A 'Merry Christmas' say the children, but that is no more for me."[2]

On Friday, December 25, 1863, Longfellow—as a 57-year-old widowed father of six children, the oldest of which had been nearly paralyzed as his country fought a war against itself—wrote a poem seeking to capture the struggle in his own heart and the world he observed around him that Christmas Day. He heard the Christmas bells ringing in Cambridge and the singing of "peace on earth." The simple sound of the church bells brought Longfellow a confident hope, even in the midst of bleak despair. He recounted to himself that God is alive, righteousness shall prevail, and peace on earth has come. In those bells and singing, he experienced good news.[3]

Now travel back to the Judean hillside just beyond Bethlehem. Imagine the scene: shepherds on the graveyard shift, waiting and watching in the stillness of the night, ears and eyes open for signs of danger, sheep bleating in the background. And then, out of nowhere, appeared an angel of the

Lord, the glory of God, and news of a promise perfectly kept, the advent of peace.

This good news announcement of peace on earth is the very thing every human heart longs to hear. We all want peace. People search tirelessly for peace. God invited these nomadic sheepherders into His story and then deployed them as the first evangelists. This was the *gospel*, a word that simply means "good news." The gospel message of peace from the angels and the arrival of the Messiah was too good and too much for the shepherds to contain. They were overwhelmed with joy and with God's glory and goodness. They experienced peace, and they were compelled to share.

Just as God called the shepherds to testify of Christ's birth, we are also called to herald that good news. We are compelled to share the saving work of His death and resurrection. This message affords mankind peace with God. Once we have encountered Christ, we become messengers of His peace.

REFLECT: How did you first hear the gospel? What fears keep you from sharing the news that Jesus has come to save sinners? Look up Colossians 1:3-6. How might the assurance in this passage increase your boldness?

RESPOND: Today, focus on His peace. Trust God and don't lean on your own understanding. Don't base your peace on the circumstances around you but on His kept promises. Let the peace of God strengthen your resolve to surrender your will to His. As Christmas approaches, keep your focus on the Prince of Peace, Who came as a Lamb.

DAY 14

A Unique Analogy: Shepherds and Sheep

He will feed his flock like a shepherd. He will carry the lambs in his arms, holding them close to his heart. He will gently lead the mother sheep with their young.
Isaiah 40:11

"God has words of strong rebuke and warning for bad shepherds, and prophecies of a good shepherd that is to come."
Mary Beth Gladwell[1]

BY THIS POINT in our journey, a reminder of its purpose is in order. Why all of this talk of Passover, of lambs and shepherds, of sheep and sacrifices? This is, after all, a Christmas devotional.

53

Of course, you can make the obvious connection with animals being around the manger in the Nativity, but you cannot read very far into the pages of Scripture before you find this shepherd-sheep motif. In the Bible, sheep are often used to illustrate people and shepherds to illustrate leaders, such as God and human kings. This unique analogy points to a deeper truth: God is using a simple picture of shepherds and sheep to point us to His own heart, to our deepest need, and to the very reason for Christmas.

WHY SHEPHERDS?

The Bible has much to say about shepherds. Abraham and Moses and David were shepherds. The Bible often paints comforting pictures of a shepherd confidently leading, feeding, protecting, and caring for his flock. And the ultimate example of this role is seen in Jesus, who is called the *Good Shepherd*. The imagery of a shepherd and his flock provide a beautiful picture of the way God cares for and nurtures His people. He guides and He guards.

WHY SHEEP?

The Bible also draws from the characteristics of sheep to apply the metaphor to people. God first compared the Israelites to sheep and later applied that label to all who are called by His name. When you consider what sheep are like, it's not the least bit surprising that God chose them to describe us, but is also not a flattering comparison. Sheep are defenseless, dumb, and extremely dependent. They are in desperate need of leadership from a shepherd. Sheep wander and fret, and they are helpless to defend themselves from predators. Consider a modern-day news story about the nature of sheep to be followers:

Hundreds of sheep followed their leader off a cliff in eastern Turkey, plunging to their deaths this week while shepherds looked on in dismay. Four hundred sheep fell 15 metres to their deaths in a ravine in Van province near Iran but broke the fall of another 1,100 animals who survived. Shepherds from a nearby village neglected the flock while eating breakfast, leaving the sheep to roam free. The loss to local farmers was estimated at $74,000.[2]

Not only are sheep mentioned in the Bible as flocks led by shepherds, but also they were used for sacrifice. Year after year, God's people offered sacrifices because of their sins. The ultimate picture of a sufficient sacrifice was Jesus Christ, the sinless Lamb Who died for sinners.

We are in desperate need of leadership from Jesus, our Good Shepherd. We are His people and the sheep of His pasture. We are in desperate need of a sufficient sacrifice for our sin. Jesus is the perfect, sinless, spotless Lamb of God, able and willing to take the sins of the world upon Himself. Jesus is the Good Shepherd who calls us sheep His sheep. Author Tim Challies eloquently sums up this beautiful relationship:

> To say that God is our shepherd and we are sheep is to humble ourselves, admitting what is true about us, and to elevate God, declaring what is true of him. When you say, "The Lord is my shepherd," you are saying something that ought to move your heart in praise and gratitude. To declare that God is your shepherd is to praise and glorify him because God the shepherd stoops down to care for poor, lost, not-so-smart sheep like you and me.[3]

REFLECT: Aren't you grateful that we have a shepherd who watches over our souls? Aren't you amazed that Jesus would die in our place and take away our sins?

RESPOND: Read 1 Peter 1:18-19: "For you know that God paid a ransom to save you from the empty life you inherited from your ancestors. And it was not paid with mere gold or silver, which lose their value. It was the precious blood of Christ, the sinless, spotless Lamb of God." Thank God for the complete forgiveness you have because of Jesus Christ, the Lamb of God.

DAY 15

The Shepherd of the Story

At that time there was a man in Jerusalem named Simeon.
He was righteous and devout and was eagerly waiting
for the Messiah to come and rescue Israel.
The Holy Spirit was upon him.
Luke 2:25

"I have seen your salvation,
which you have prepared for all people.
He is a light to reveal God to the nations,
and he is the glory of your people Israel!"
Simeon, Luke 2:30-32

THE PEOPLE of God had groped in darkness with a longing for rescue. They could not find their way out of the darkness. They were helpless but not altogether hopeless. The promises of deliverance were there, but God had been silent for some time, and those promises seemed distant. It is easy to imagine their hopes faded and grew dim at times. "Hope deferred makes the heart sick," we are told in Proverbs 13:12. Sometimes, the longer we wait, the less we hope.

The people of that day are not unlike us. The pressures of our lives can squeeze out hopeful expectations. We go through the motions of life and wonder if there is any consolation, any relief, any hope. Have difficult seasons of life ever drained hope from you? The people of God were there, and hope was waning.

God's promised Messiah had been a long time coming—a very long time. Some waited with more eager expectation than others. In Luke 2, we meet two such people, Simeon and Anna. These two held out firm hope that God would help His people. They prayed He would arrive in their lifetime and eagerly awaiting the arrival of the Shepherd of the story, who would lead the people out of darkness and into God's light.

The people of Israel were waiting for the consolation of their nation and expecting the redemption of Jerusalem. They knew the Messiah, a Savior, was on the way because God had promised repeatedly throughout Scripture. The Messiah was to be born in Bethlehem (Micah 5:2) to a virgin (Isaiah 7:14). He would come out of Egypt (Hosea 11:1) and be called a Nazarene (Isaiah 11:1). He would be the Son of God (Psalm 2:12, Proverbs 30:4) and yet God Himself (Isaiah 9:6-7, Jeremiah 23:5-6, Zechariah 2:10). He would heal lepers and open the eyes of the blind, and the lame would leap for joy (Isaiah

35:5-6). His hands and feet would be pierced (Psalm 22:17), and He would be mocked, ridiculed, and tortured before his execution. He would be a suffering servant (Isaiah 53:4-8).

The Messiah would also be a shepherd. Ezekiel 34 offers prophetic imagery of shepherds and sheep, pointing to shepherds who were overseers for the people of God and to another shepherd who was to come later. By calling himself the Good Shepherd, Jesus laid claim to the Old Testament promises that foretold the Messiah.

Simeon and Anna were righteous in their living, grounded in Scripture and focused on God. They knew Jesus was the long-awaited shepherd. Messiah had arrived. Let's examine few important lessons from Simeon and Anna: (1) They hoped in patient faith. Sometimes, waiting can be the most painful place for us to be. Yet in the waiting, our faith is developed and our surrender to the Lord is deepened. (2) The frailty of their age points to their helpless lot and to God's good mercy. God's grace meets us at the end of our own resources. (3) Jesus arrived after a time of silent centuries. Heaven had been tightly shut, yet at just the right time, the Shepherd of the story appeared. In the darkest of times, God shines light on our lives. He is our Good Shepherd who leads us out of the darkness.

REFLECT: Are you trying to work your way out of a dark situation rather than trusting in and waiting for the Lord? Are you growing tired of waiting for relief and losing hope? Search out promises God has for you in His Word, especially the excellent gifts He gives through Christ, the Shepherd of the story.

RESPOND: Gracious Heavenly Father, You know that I find it hard to be patient. I confess this to you today and ask for the forgiveness I have in Christ. I also ask that by Your Spirit You will help me be more patient as I wait upon You.

DAY 16

The Shepherd of Our Souls

The Lord is my shepherd;
I have all that I need.
Psalm 23:1

"Want to change your life?
Begin by saying, 'The Lord is my shepherd.'"
Max Lucado[1]

YESTERDAY, we considered how Simeon and Anna had waited for God's promised deliverance and guidance to arrive. They had listened for the voice of God their entire lives, clung to His promises because they knew His voice, and trusted His heart. They related to God in the same intimate bond that exists between sheep and shepherd. That relationship demands trust. Sheep grow to trust their shepherd. The shepherd demonstrates trustworthiness, and, over time, that builds their faith in him.

God created us in such a way. We need shepherding. That requires trusting Him. The Bible boldly asserts that "it is impossible to please God without faith."[2] Easier said than done, right? Trusting God can be scary. Letting go of the reins of control is counterintuitive for us. Running away (or running the show) seems more natural to us. We scramble to make sense of life around us. Without God, we are groping in darkness like the people of God in Simeon and Anna's day. Scattered, divided, and lost are descriptors of a shepherdless flock, and an all too apt description of a person's life without Christ.

Enter the Shepherd of our souls. As the Good Shepherd, Jesus sought us out and laid down His life for us. Christ emptied Himself, entered our condition, and pursued us in our helpless state. Jesus, our Lord and Shepherd, does not merely look down on our sorrow from a distance in pity. The Christmas narrative is about Jesus entering our suffering. As one of us and in empathy toward us, He became our *Emmanuel*, God with us.

Jesus brings us to Himself as His flock, and He is the Shepherd to us. He knows exactly where we are and what we need. Because God created you and me, He knows the actual condition of our being. He truly understands us. God knows why it is so difficult for us to love or trust someone. He is aware of our hurts, our fears, our dreams and aspirations.

The fact that He knows what you need adds a depth of rich beauty to the twenty-third Psalm. This ancient song was written by one who knew about shepherds and sheep. David tended flocks and talked to the Lord. I envision him looking over flock and field and the Holy Spirit inspiring him to contemplate the goodness of God as the Shepherd of David's soul.

This timeless song deals with the realities of life and our deepest need: the need of a Shepherd for our souls. David, the shepherd, now acknowledges his place in the care of the Good Shepherd. In a sermon on this famed text, pastor E.V. Hill passionately inquired of David, "Tell me, little lamb, about your shepherd."[3] David sang of the wisdom, strength, kindness, and power of God—his Shepherd. His opening refrain, "The Lord is my shepherd; I have all that I need," oozes trust and contentment.

God is our Shepherd in times of trouble or when we are losing heart.

God is our Shepherd in times of weariness and frustration.

God is our Shepherd when we need rest and refreshing.

God is our Shepherd when we face enemies.

As Shepherd, God does not stand calling from the other side of the valley of death… nor does He push us through. Sing again this stanza of David, "YOU ARE WITH ME."[4]

REFLECT: Consider the fact that Jesus came as the Good Shepherd and laid down His life for the sheep. He is best suited to understand us because He also became the sinless, spotless sacrificial lamb. Ponder the depth of His love and the comfort of His guidance.

RESPOND: Lord Jesus, we love You. We praise You that, for all eternity, You will be our eternal Shepherd who guides us to springs of living water. Hallelujah, You will wipe away all our tears and You will guide us into the enjoyment of Yourself for eternity. Amen.

DAY 17

Response to the Shepherd's Pursuit

My sheep listen to my voice; I know them, and they follow
me. I give them eternal life, and they will never perish.
No one can snatch them away from me.
John 10:27-28

*"Jesus seeks those whose backs are towards him, who are going
further and further away from the fold;
herein is grace most free, most full, most sovereign."*
Charles Haddon Spurgeon[1]

GROWING UP IN A MINISTRY HOME, my kids were often in and around crowds of people. My wife and I would constantly watch them to see how they reacted when they lost sight of us. We noticed that when they were separated from us in a crowd, they learned to scan the room and spot us quickly. Over time, I could snap my fingers in a certain rhythm, or even say "psssst, psssst," and they would recognize the sounds as being from me. To this day, I can get their attention in a noisy environment because of this familiarity.

I love the imagery of a shepherd calling out to his sheep, coaxing them along. His persistent gentle persuasion guides them to greener pastures or to a place of rest and safety.

Their reaction to the shepherd's voice is unlike their instinct. When sheep feel threatened, anxious, or harried, they have limited defensive responses: they huddle together or scatter. As the shepherd gently leads them along, the flock come to know and recognize the shepherd's voice and words. They follow with trust and contentment. His voice is comforting, not frightening.

Similarly, the shepherds in the fields of Bethlehem heard the call of God's voice ringing beautifully through the song of the angels. Every instinctual reaction would have been abject terror. Can you imagine the blaze of radiant light, the thundering sound of the angelic choir announcing Messiah's birth? The angel reassured them, telling them not to fear. Fear would be understandable, yet they responded with amazement, trust, and joy. Why? God made Himself clear to them.

Jesus says, "My sheep listen to my voice... and they follow me."[2] It is fascinating to me that Jesus referred to people as sheep and Himself as the Good Shepherd, but the comparison shouldn't surprise me. We aren't always the most rational beings. We spook easily and definitely need guidance. At times, we are selfish and blindly unaware of the dangers around us.

Sheep may not be too bright, but they'll trust a shepherd they know. If someone they don't know tries to herd them, they will run away in fear. However, when they hear the voice and words they know, they respond with confidence and trust.

Many people run from the voice of the Shepherd. They don't understand His loving care and compassion. They don't comprehend His character and the lengths to which Christ has gone to save them.

God's passionate pursuit of us involved sending His beloved Son to die in our place. Because we could not reach Him through our own efforts, He reached down to us. Jesus taught of a shepherd leaving the ninety-nine and searching for the one lost sheep. God pursues us, even when we are obstinate, resistant, and even hiding.

Just as a shepherd will search diligently for a sheep that finds itself separated from the flock until he finds it, so Jesus sought for the lost. Romans 5:8 (NIV) says, "But God demonstrates his own love for us in this: While we were still sinners, Christ died for us." He pursues with gentle love and compassion and a demonstration of His love. Today, respond to the voice of the Good Shepherd, Jesus Christ. He is lovingly pursuing you.

REFLECT: In this Advent season, Jesus, the Good Shepherd, is calling to us. Do you hear his voice? Will you listen and follow Him? Are you making room for God in your life so you can hear His voice? Is His voice being constantly drowned out by the competing voices of the world? It is easy to be constantly distracted by other voices, lesser voices.

RESPOND: Spend time in prayer today listening to His voice. Make time for His Word. Prayer for today: Lord, thank You for pursuing me with Your great love and compassion. Thank You for making yourself fully known in Christ Jesus. Teach me to learn and listen to Your voice. In Jesus' Name, amen.

DAY 18

Movement Toward God

When the angels had returned to heaven, the shepherds said
to each other, "Let's go to Bethlehem! Let's see this thing that
has happened, which the Lord has told us about."
Luke 2:15-16

"It's good to be in a hurry if you are excited
about something that really matters.
Nothing in all the world matters more than the birth of Jesus."
Ray Pritchard[1]

MONOTONY... that might well sum up the nature of life for a night-watching shepherd, each night numbingly familiar and painfully repeatable—gentle breezes, blinding darkness (except for the twinkling of stars), deafening silence (except for the soft, distant bleating of the flock or the crackle of a fire), and a longing for daylight.

Most interruptions to this well-worn routine were unwelcome. A disturbance to the silence likely meant a wayward sheep or a would-be predator. But this was not just any interruption; it was a divine invasion. Blazing, dazzling lights pierced the darkness of the night sky. An angel appeared. Pastor Mark Dunn said, "It was nothing less than the glory of God, reflected in the radiance of one of His holy messengers."[2] Hours of silent routine were shattered by something unimaginable. Ordinarily, fight-or-flight responses might kick in, but this angelic appearance was so overwhelming, I cannot imagine a will to fight in this moment. Such a terrifying experience would doubtless cause most to run.

In fact, the angel first "reassured them... Don't be afraid!"[3] This was the night of the Savior's birth. This was the most glorious good news ever told. The darkness of the shepherds' night had been broken by the radiance of the angel of the Lord, and the darkness of sin's curse was now overshadowed by the Light of Life.

The angel gave them the good news that a Savior, who is Christ the Lord, was born unto them in the city of David. They watched and listened as the entire night sky erupted in rapturous song by an angelic choir from heaven. The theme of the song was the glory of God; the promise of the song, peace on Earth.

The song ended. The angels left. Darkness returned. But the shepherds would never be the same. The angels went back into heaven, but they left behind some light—the light of the knowledge of the glory of God in the face of Jesus Christ.[4]

In awe of this spectacular announcement, the shepherds were moved to action. They responded, "Let's go to Bethlehem! Let's see this thing that has happened." They simply could not stay in the fields. They were compelled to go and see, so they hurried off. Maybe they ran all the way into town. Maybe they sang the angels' song as they went. We can't know those things for certain, but we know the birth of Christ is an invitation to move toward God.

In Bethlehem, the shepherds would discover the most astonishing event in human history and see for themselves Almighty God incarnated in the person of an infant named Jesus. God came down, and He invited them to draw near. God came down, and He extends that same invitation today. He calls us to leave the familiar, the comfortable, the routine. God calls us to experience the supernatural. He calls us to paths we've never walked before. He calls us to Himself.

REFLECT: We get in a hurry for so many things these days, especially as Christmas approaches. We hurry to buy gifts, formulate menus, and keep schedules. Hurry isn't always bad, though—not if we're hurrying to do the right things. The shepherds hurried toward God. Are you in a hurry to move toward God or away from Him?

RESPOND: Move closer to God today. *Get still, get quiet.* Stop the unnecessary hurry. Make space for God to speak. Stop the unnecessary noise. Turn off the TV. Put down your phone. Pick up your Bible. Take time today to reflect on Luke 2. Read it slowly and prayerfully. James 4:8 says, "Come close to God, and God will come close to you."

DAY 19

G lory

The shepherds went back to their flocks,
glorifying and praising God for all they had heard and seen.
It was just as the angel had told them.
Luke 2:20

Go, tell it on the mountain;
Over the hills and everywhere
Go, tell it on the mountain
That Jesus Christ is born.[1]

HAVE you ever been really excited about something, only to develop a serious case of buyer's remorse or post-event blues afterward? I often think about the anticipation of big moments in my life. I work and I wait with excitement, hanging my hopes on some upcoming event or experience.

Many times, just as high as the buildup can take me, the letdown can be just as low.

We plan and prepare for months for the perfect Christmas: festive gatherings with the ideal menu, guest list, and just the right gifts for everyone. But the days after Christmas can be blue. The gift may not live up to the hype, or the family dynamics were less than warm and fuzzy. The long-awaited day on the calendar came and went, and instead of reveling in exuberance, you spiral downward in disappointment.

These letdowns are not just an after-holiday slump. They are part of a phenomenon that touches other areas of life: postpartum depression, buyer's remorse, or a simple case of unmet expectations.

After all the decorations are down and the guests say goodbye and the leftovers are long gone, we return to "normal" (whatever that is). But not the shepherds. Yes, they did return, but they did not go back the same. And nothing would ever be normal for them again. They were profoundly impacted by the glory of God and all that the angel had told them.

Their journey of returning is fascinating. Three primary questions emerge: *How* did they return? *From what* did they return? And *to what* did they return?

How did they return? First, the Bible says they returned "glorifying and praising God." They returned, recounting all they'd heard and seen. They returned with an overwhelming hunger to tell it. This same word, *praising*, was used of the angels' song. This was probably a song, too. The shepherds' hearts were bursting with His glory, and they erupted in praise.

From what did they return? The shepherds returned from a life-changing, face-to-face encounter with the Living God.

Angels had told them the Christ was born, and that's exactly what they hurried off to see. The simple testimony of Scripture is that "It was just as the angel had told them."[2] So much is implanted in that one sentence. Notice that verse again: "It was just as the angel had told them."[3] What was *it*?

It was the dawning of hope; the *it* was the redemption of man. *It* was God incarnate, the Savior of the world. They were in the presence of the Promised Redeemer, God's Messiah, Emmanuel. They had seen Jesus, and that's why they returned "glorifying and praising God."

An encounter with Christ leads to a visible difference. The shepherds experienced the character and nature of God. They were in the presence of holiness, which radiates to the ends of the earth in glory.

Alex Motyer defines the relationship this way: "Holiness is God's hidden glory: glory is God's all-present holiness."[4] God is intrinsically holy and perfect; that holiness on display is called glory. A glimpse of the glory of this God is simply manifested holiness.

The shepherds couldn't contain their praise, and they boldly shared the good news. They were so excited about their significant discovery that they couldn't keep it to themselves. That leads us to the third question: *To what did they return?* They went back to the fields, back to the sheep, back to their jobs, their struggles, their burdens, and their temptations. In other words, they went back to their everyday responsibilities. They returned to the demands of shepherding, but now with a wholly new perspective. This encounter with the Living God changed everything for them. And it will change everything for you, too.

Our prayer for every reader of these devotionals is that you have a personal relationship with the Lord Jesus. We pray you would repent of your sins and, by faith, commit your life to Christ. If you've already done that, we pray that you would have a fresh encounter with Jesus that will impact the way you live in the ordinary routines of your responsibilities. We pray that your life would reflect His glory.

REFLECT: Can the people around you (your family members, your neighbors, your coworkers or classmates) see that you have been with Jesus? One of the first evidences of a genuine, soul-stirring, life-changing encounter with the living God is a hunger to give Him glory and a burning heart to share His glory with others. Is that true of you?

RESPOND: If you have not been with Jesus, you can change that situation right now if you're willing to repent of your sins and commit your life to Him in faith. If you'll reach out to Him by meeting those two conditions, you'll receive his matchless gift of eternal life. You can explore this more at 41series.com/newlife.

DAY 20

P raise

The shepherds went back to their flocks,
glorifying and praising God for all they had heard and seen.
It was just as the angel had told them.
Luke 2:20

"You are writing a gospel, a page each day,
By the things you do, and the things you say;
Men are reading that gospel, whether faultless or true;
Say, what is the gospel according to you?"
Paul Gilbert[1]

THE INVITATION of Christmas is a call to praise. The good news (gospel) message of Christmas is a call to worship. I get goosebumps every time I think about the shock and holy awe the shepherds must have experienced in the presence of heavenly hosts singing praises to God. Luminous angelic beings filled the night sky over shepherd's fields, echoing a chorus of praise that proclaimed the call of Christmas. This was a call to praise.

The shepherds not only answered that call; they extended it to others. Luke records, "After seeing him, the shepherds told everyone what had happened and what the angel had said to them about this child. All who heard the shepherds' story were astonished."[2]

Luke's gospel tells us that after meeting the Christ-child, the shepherds returned to their flocks. And they did so with a song of praise. They couldn't contain their praise. They were compelled to share and took the message of the gospel back to their world.

What a powerful reminder for us all. We will not see God's Kingdom established (on earth as it is in heaven) while remaining separated from those around us. We cannot sit in holy huddles in churches and neglect to go and tell. Jesus deserves our highest and loudest praise. We take steps to make the Kingdom a reality in our world by living our lives for the praise of Christ in everyday, ordinary places. In other words, we go back to our families and friends, to our jobs and schools, to our neighbors, and to the nations to tell the story of the good news of Jesus. Our praise becomes a call for others to join in praise. The praises of our lives should be a recruiting tool for others to join the choir.

After these Christmas holidays are over, keep the call of Christmas before you. Continue to praise the Lord by loving others well and by sharing Jesus as the One who came to save us. The angels praised the One whom God had sent, and the shepherds praised the One whom they met in the manger. Like the angels and the shepherds, we can tell the story of

Jesus as we go about our days and our routines of life. Make every day peppered with praise, and others will notice. Some will join in. Some will not. Their response is not your responsibility. You and I are simply called to praise the Lord.

Praise is our *calling* (1 Corinthians 10:31). Praise is a *commission* (Psalm 150:6). And praise is our *celebration* of the greatness of our God. We ascribe infinite worth to our God in a lifestyle of praise. Worship is far more than song. We acknowledge His worth to us in everyday, common ways. Praise is expressed in our gratitude and in our attitude. You and I can express praise to God in the management of our time, our money, our relationships, and how we use our gifts, talents, experiences, and abilities. Charles Spurgeon said, "Praise is the rehearsal of our eternal song. By grace we learn to sing, and in glory we continue to sing."[3]

REFLECT: What helps you to praise God? Reflect on the idea of Christmas as a call to praise. How can your praise extend that call to others? How does the greatness of God impact your worship?

RESPOND: Father, I pray that this Christmas, we would be people who carry the good news of Jesus to all peoples. May our lives amplify this call to praise Jesus. He is worthy of all praise. Thank You, Father, for the heavenly hosts and for the shepherds that praised You during that first Advent. Thank You, Father, that we can join in this song of praise that will continue throughout eternity. In Jesus' Name, amen.

DAY 21

J oy

Anna, a prophet, was also there in the Temple…
She came along just as Simeon was talking with Mary and
Joseph, and she began praising God. She talked about the
child to everyone who had been waiting expectantly
for God to rescue Jerusalem.
Luke 2:36-38

"Joy is distinctly a Christian word and a Christian thing.
It is the reverse of happiness.
Happiness is the result of what happens of an agreeable sort.
Joy has its springs deep down inside.
And that spring never runs dry, no matter what happens.
Only Jesus gives that joy."
S.D. Gordon[1]

I LOVE CHRISTMAS MUSIC. Without apology, I could listen to it year round. And either you are with me, or you're wrong about this matter (I said what I said). By this point in the Advent season, the songs of Christmas fill the airwaves. Many radio stations have even gone to a twenty-four-hour Christmas fest. GLORY! (Amen, anyone?)

I've noticed that many of the songs we sing at Christmastime are reminders of the implied happiness of the holiday: "It's the Most Wonderful Time of the Year," "Have a Holly Jolly Christmas," and "Walking in a Winter Wonderland" all communicate a joyous, trouble-free state of mind.

But if you are honest, that may not be what you are experiencing this season. I've come to realize that Christmas for many people isn't the most wonderful time of the year; in fact, it can be the most difficult time of the year. Some are missing children, parents, or other loved ones. Some people won't make it home for Christmas ever again. Although the world has moved on past the COVID pandemic in many ways, some are still stuck in a place of isolation.

Many just want the season all to be over because it's too painful to be force fed pictures of joy, when everyday life is a struggle. For many this Christmastime, the world does not look like a winter wonderland. It just looks like winter.

We've already mentioned that hyped expectations about what Christmas is supposed to be can bring disappointment and disillusionment when the real thing doesn't measure up. So how can we improve our level of joy this Christmas? One answer is found in the story of the Anna in Luke 2.

Here is a woman who spent her life waiting and watching, trusting and tarrying. She spent decades of her life in the temple, praying, fasting, and worshipping. Anna understood that joy was rooted in the character and promises of

God, especially as they are related and revealed to us in Christ.

Once she saw Jesus, two things happened. First, praise flowed naturally. Her response to the Messiah was to continue what she had been doing. She had praised God for years based upon the promise of what would come. She now praised God for the promise kept. This is a signpost of joy. It is an inside job. Joy is sustaining. Her joy was not based on circumstances, but on Christ.

Second, the text says she "talked about the child to everyone who had been waiting expectantly for God to rescue Jerusalem." Her joy was multiplied by others who held the same anticipation and trust in God. Joy is a kind of happiness, but it does not depend on what is happening. There were many nameless people alongside Simeon and Anna, who held out great hope for God to bring deliverance... and now it was realized. Joy had sustained them in waiting and now filled them as they worshipped.

Anna and Simeon (and others who waited expectantly) were seeking God's fulfillment. Your level of joy at Christmas is directly related to what it is you seek. If you're simply looking for fun and festivities and feel goods, then Christmas happiness may evaporate as quickly as appears. If you look for joy in the wrong places this Christmas, you might be left with emptiness. Oh, that this Christmas, you would seek a fresh glimpse of He who was born to be the redemption of Israel—the Lamb of God who takes away the sin of the world. Seek Him and you will find Him... and in finding Him, you will find joy.

Jesus offers true, lasting joy, a joy that surpasses all worldly pleasures and sustains during all of life. Jesus gives joy that sustains us through trials, hardships, tragedies, and periods of waiting. His joy lasts forever. We find this joy in Christ by beholding by faith the beauty of God's grace and love for us in Christ. Someone has said that life can put joy in jail, but joy can find joy in jail.

REFLECT: What do you seek this Christmas? Are you content with a search for happiness, or are you expecting joy? Where are you looking for joy? What are some practical examples of how you can choose joy today, even during difficult circumstances?

RESPOND: In the natural, we focus on circumstances. In the supernatural, we focus on Jesus. Make a list of things that Jesus has given you right now that tomorrow cannot touch.

DAY 22

Pointing to the Lamb Who Saves

The passage of Scripture he had been reading was this: "He
was led like a sheep to the slaughter. And as a lamb is silent
before the shearers, He did not open his mouth.
In His humiliation He was deprived of justice.
Who can speak of his descendants?
For his life was taken from the earth."
Acts 8:32-33

*"All preaching must point to His sin-bearing, substitutionary death
for sinners. All exposition must lift up this Sacrificial Lamb who
became a sin-bearing substitute for all who believe. Every message
must exalt this Christ, who was raised from the dead,
exalted to the right hand of God the Father,
and entrusted with all authority in heaven and earth."*
Steven J. Lawson[1]

This concept of Jesus as the Lamb of God appears throughout Scripture. The Passover lambs who were slain all point to the Passover Lamb who saves. The concept of Jesus as the Passover Lamb is found uniquely in the book of Acts.

In Acts 8, Philip had been sent by an angel down the road that ran from Jerusalem to Gaza. Philip met the treasurer of Ethiopia, a eunuch. This eunuch worshipped in Jerusalem and was returning in his carriage. As he was riding, he was reading the book of Isaiah. Of all the Scriptures he could have been reading, he was reading Isaiah 53:7-8. This man was reading about the future Lamb who would be slain.

Philip asked him if he understood what he was reading. The eunuch replied, "How can I, unless someone instructs me?" We all need guidance in reading Scripture. It is wise to seek wisdom from others, especially in the difficult passages found in the Bible. So Philip climbed in the carriage, and they fellowshipped around the Word of God. The encounter continues in Acts 8:34-35: "The eunuch asked Philip, 'Tell me, please, who is the prophet talking about, himself or someone else?' Then Philip began with that very passage of Scripture and told him the good news about Jesus."

The encounter between Philip and the eunuch from Africa is intriguing on several levels. First, this teaching was very unusual during the time of the early church. Dr. Richard Longenecker says, "A doctrine of a suffering Messiah was unheard of and considered unthinkable in first-century Jewish religious circles."[2] It was unthinkable to them that the Savior would suffer. Jesus was unlike anyone they had ever fathomed. Rather than rescue by rule, Jesus served through suffering. Second, the Ethiopian asked if the prophet was talking about himself or someone else. Philip told him the Good News about Jesus. The eunuch asked a question, and

Philip took him straight to the gospel of Jesus Christ. Pointing to the Lamb who saves is always a great idea during any witnessing encounter.

However, I wonder how long that conversation lasted and what Scriptures Philip expounded. The man of God took the Word of God and led him to the Lamb of God. Whatever happened in that carriage, the eunuch was so convicted that he immediately took the next step of baptism.

Here is a man who kept the treasury of the queen of Ethiopia. Little did he know that morning as he went to worship that he would discover the greatest treasure in the world. He had held the treasures of Ethiopia in his hand; this day, he would finally hold the treasure of heaven in his heart. He went to worship, but left reading the Word. Going to church wasn't enough for him. He needed more of God than just what he got at worship, so he was reading God's Word. As a eunuch, he had suffered physically to be set apart. He had gone through great lengths to ensure his physical desires would be diminished. On this day, he would discover that only a relationship with God can spiritually set a person apart. Only a heart decision for Jesus releases the power of God over the temptations of your life.

REFLECT: Philip was obedient to the leading of the Spirit, and the eunuch responded to God and was baptized. Consider the words of pastor and author R. Kent Hughes: "There are all kinds of 'chance' meetings ready to take place in a life that is sensitive and obedient to God's leading."[3]

RESPOND: How can you be sensitive to the Spirit's leading in your life today? Make sure not to miss any of the divine appointments that God has for you.

DAY 23

P reaching to the Lost Sheep

Jesus sent out the twelve apostles with these instructions:
"Don't go to the Gentiles or the Samaritans,
but only to the people of Israel —God's lost sheep."
Matthew 10:5-6

*"In order to move from comfortable Christianity to a Matthew 10
kind of Christianity, I want to suggest two prayers that we ought
to be praying. First, **God, give us supernatural awareness of the
condition of the lost**. We need help to see what God sees. We need
to see it in the people right around us, the people we work with and
live among, and the people who surround us in the world. . .
Our second prayer should be this: **God, give us sacrificial
obedience to the commission of Christ.**"*
David Platt[1]

I ENJOY WATCHING the Summer Olympics. My favorite event is the men's 4x100m relay. It is exciting watching a race for which nations send their four fastest athletes to compete against each other in a footrace to the finish. You would think it was all about the pure speed and athletic ability of the runners, yet the most important part of this race is the ability to pass along the baton. In an event the winner is determined by tenths of a second, the exchange of the baton is an extremely critical part of the race. The ability to pass the baton is fundamental to the success of a track team,

Likewise, our ability as followers of Jesus Christ to pass on the Good News is critical in the race of the Christian life. It will not matter how fast we have run our race or how far we have gone in our Christian life if we do not successfully pass on the message of Jesus Christ to the next generation. There is much more than an Olympic medal at stake. If we do not successfully share our faith, we could be one generation away from an entire world who doesn't know Jesus Christ. The ability to pass on the gospel of Christ is fundamental to being true followers of Jesus Christ.

Matthew 10 records when God sent out the twelve apostles. The word for apostle comes from the root word *apostello* in the original Greek language. *Apostello* means "to commission or send forth." The word focuses back on the authority of the one giving the commission. Thus, the twelve apostles are "sent out ones" who carry the authority of the One sending them: Jesus Christ.

God clearly sent His disciples with the Good News to the entire world. But He also clearly started with His chosen people, the nation of Israel. This is the well-defined strategy repeated in Acts 1:8: "But you will receive power when the Holy Spirit comes on you; and you will be my witnesses in

Jerusalem, and in all Judea and Samaria, and to the ends of the earth." God wants His message shared around the world, but He wants us to start at home.

In this world full of lost sheep, we have the best news of all. The Good News is that death has been conquered, sin has been covered, Satan has been condemned, and hell is a choice. You don't have to spend eternity separated from God. You can choose to accept the Good News of eternal life with Jesus Christ.

Aren't you glad that somebody cared enough about you to share Jesus? I am so thankful for my wife, wise friends, parents, and preachers who passed on the Good News of Christ to me. I am eternally grateful that they didn't drop the baton!

Sometimes people use excuses for why they don't share their faith. I have heard the following remarks often: "I just can't talk well" or "I don't know what to say." Yet people have no problem talking about anything they love or care about. It is not about your ability to speak or communicate; it is about the passion and priority of your life. If Jesus is the priority of your life and you love Him more than anything else, passing on the Good News about Him should be second nature. God has sent us out with his gospel to pass to the next generation. May we not drop His baton.

REFLECT and RESPOND: Let us pass on the gospel of Jesus Christ and go faithfully as His "sent out ones." May the following quote inspire you to make this life count for His glory: "This is our time on the history line of God. This is it. What will we do with the one deep exhale of God on this earth? For we are but a vapor and we have to make it count. We're on. Direct us, Lord, and get us on our feet."[2]

DAY 24

A Warning about Pretending Prophets

"Beware of false prophets
who come disguised as harmless sheep
but are really vicious wolves."
Matthew 7:15

"The essence of false religion is a Christian being involved in
religious activity while being void of spiritual intimacy.
It is exemplified by a person having a ritual of religion without a
relationship with God."
Dr. Tony Evans[1]

THERE IS a world full of people who live fake lives. One thing social media has proven is that anybody can play-act. It is easy to only show the world what you want others to see. Millions of people on social media hide behind the pretense that everything in their world is flawless when their lives are far from fulfilled. The real world of struggles lies just outside their profile photos and perfect-world posts.

The world in Jesus' day was very similar, just without the opportunity to post it all online. The religious elite in Jesus' day worried more about their reputation with other leaders than they did about their right standing with the Lord. It was easy for them to wear boxes with Scripture on their forehead while not having His Word hidden in their hearts. They could wear long tassels symbolizing their obedience to the law while living lives short on grace. They could pray public prayers that sounded full of insight but still be blinded to God's will. The religious elite were the professional play actors of the day. The Message Bible paraphrases Jesus' words in Matthew 6:1-3:

> Be especially careful when you are trying to be good so that you don't make a performance out of it. It might be good theater, but the God who made you won't be applauding. When you do something for someone else, don't call attention to yourself. You've seen them in action, I'm sure —'playactors' I call them—treating prayer meeting and street corner alike as a stage, acting compassionate as long as someone is watching, playing to the crowds. They get applause, true, but that's all they get.

One would think it would be hard enough to live in a world full of pretending people and self-righteous leaders.

Then, throw into that mix the spectacle of false preachers. This was a combination worthy of God's warning. In Matthew 7:15-20 (TM), Jesus warned about preachers who don't practice what they preach:

> Be wary of false preachers who smile a lot, dripping with practiced sincerity. Chances are they are out to rip you off in some way or other. Don't be impressed with charisma; look for character. Who preachers *are* is the main thing, not what they say. A genuine leader will never exploit your emotions or your pocketbook. These diseased trees with their bad apples are going to be chopped down and burned (TM).

Jesus claims these false prophets pretend to be harmless sheep, but they are actually vicious wolves. Envision yourself at a nice restaurant, ordering lamb. However, instead of biting into tender lamb, you take a bite of wolf. Wow, that would be a shock to your system! Jesus says in Matthew 7:16, "By their fruit you will recognize them." False people cannot bear anything but fake fruit. And fake fruit is easy to recognize because it never passes the taste test.

It is in this context of Scripture that Jesus gives what I believe are the most frightening words in the Bible in Matthew 7:21-23:

> Not everyone who says to Me, "Lord, Lord," will enter the kingdom of heaven, but only the one who does the will of My Father who is in heaven. Many will say to Me on that day, "Lord, Lord, did we not prophesy in Your name and in Your name drive out demons and in Your name perform many miracles?" Then I will tell them plainly, "I never knew you. Away from Me, you evildoers!"

That warning gives us a reality check on what is real in our spiritual lives and what it not.

REFLECT: Consider Ivor Powell's words about Matthew 7:15: "Religion is not righteousness; preaching is not proof of godliness."[2] How do you stay pure in a world that pretends? How can you recognize the fake fruit of false leaders?

RESPOND: Pray for God to reveal what is pure in your life. Pray also for Him to expose clearly any areas where you are pretending.

DAY 25

A Powerful Description of Judgment

"But when the Son of Man comes in His glory, and all the
angels with Him, then He will sit upon His glorious
throne. All the nations will be gathered in His presence, and
He will separate the people as a shepherd separates the sheep
from the goats. He will place the sheep at His right hand and
the goats at His left."
Matthew 25:31-33

"The entire New Testament is overshadowed by the certainty
of a coming day of universal judgment,
and by the problem thence arising:
how may we sinners get right with God
while there is yet time?"
J. I. Packer[1]

MATTHEW 25 CONTAINS three teachings revolving around the return of Jesus Christ: the parable of the ten virgins (vv. 1-13), the parable of the talents (vv. 14-30), and a comparison between the sheep and the goats (vv. 31-46). In the metaphor of the sheep and goats, Jesus compares how a shepherd of His day separated sheep from goats to how the Chief Shepherd will one day separate the saved and the lost.

There is spiritual significance as to why Jesus compares sheep to saved people and goats to lost people. To this day in the Middle East, sheep and goats regularly graze together but need to be separated at night so that the goats, being less hardy, can be kept warm. It's often quite difficult to tell them apart. They can be similar in color, but one main difference is that the sheep's tail hangs down and the goat's sticks up.[2]

Like wheat and tares, they look similar until separated. The difference in sheep and goats lies on what is found on the inside. Sheep know the Shepherd in a personal way. Goats don't know the Shepherd's voice. They walk around with their tails in the air, full of stubbornness and pride. Therefore, when Jesus returns to judge the world, He will divide all mankind into two groups, labeled as sheep and goats.

Matthew 25:34-40 explains Jesus' conversation with the saved, while verses 41-45 describe His exchange with the lost. The main difference between these two groups is identified in verses 40 and 45. To the saved Jesus will say, "Truly I tell, whatever you did for one of the least of mine, you did it for Me." To the lost, Jesus will proclaim, "Truly I tell you, whatever you did not do for one of the least of these, you did not do for Me." Jesus makes a clear connection between the works of true believers. Those who are truly saved by grace are saved to do good works. What we believe shows up in how we behave. When Jesus returns, the determining factor will not be our talk, but our walk. Did we live out what we say we believed?

The Shepherd will one day divide His sheep from the world's goats. I find it extremely enlightening that the names of all saved people are found in a book entitled the Lamb's Book of Life. Revelation 13:8 (NIV) says, "All inhabitants of the earth will worship the beast—all whose names have not been written in the Lamb's Book of Life, the Lamb who was slain from the creation of the world." So the Shepherd's sheep have their names written in the Lamb's book of life. And Scripture warns in the very next verse, "Whoever has ears, let them hear."

One day, God is going to lead His sheep out. There is no getting out of it. The Lamb of God will return as the Lion of the tribe of Judah. His Second Coming is imminent and His judgment impending. There will be a division of all people into two groups. The world will not be divided by skin color, nationality, job descriptions, bank account balances, or past sins. There will be just two groups of people: saved and lost. That will be the only thing that matters that day. It should then be the only thing that matters to us every day. Nothing is more important than your personal relationship with God's Lamb.

REFLECT and RESPOND: Seriously consider Jesus' ending statement in Matthew 25:46: "Then they will go away to eternal punishment, but the righteous to eternal life." What group are you in? How do you know? Are you prepared for His return?

DAY 26

A lmost Time

When Jesus had finished saying all these things,
He said to His disciples, "As you know, Passover begins in
two days, and the Son of Man will be handed over to be
crucified."
Matthew 26:1-2

*"Several hundred thousand lambs were herded
through the streets of Jerusalem every Passover."*
Flavius Josephus[1]

ON THE DAY I am writing this devotion, my wife and I spent a
great day together at the beach. As I watched the waves roll
in, it reminded me of the repetition and consistency of God's
use of a lamb in Scripture. As you watch one wave roll into

shore and look behind it, another is on the way. One wave crashes the beach, and right behind it, another. The 104 references to a lamb in God's Word occur the same way. As soon as you study one analogy of a lamb and it lands in the center of your heart, you continue looking in Scripture and another follows close behind.

As we have watched several waves of God's truth roll in, we come to one gigantic wave after another as we enter the Passover and Passion week. Theologian James Montgomery Boice describes the scene in Matthew 26:2:

> For twenty-five chapters, ever since the introduction of Jesus as the descendant of David in verse 1 of chapter 1, the story of Christ's life has been moving toward a powerful, gripping climax: the murder of the King followed by His resurrection. The story started slowly, but it has been building in intensity throughout the three-year ministry and has now reached the point where the final act of the drama is at hand. The King has come to Jerusalem for the final time, and the leaders of the people, who hate Him, are plotting His arrest and execution.[2]

All the waves of God's matchless grace repeatedly move toward the shore of Jesus' crucifixion. Scripture after Scripture about the Passover lambs hit the ground of our faith in His final week. We call it Passion Week. Jews called it Passover. There is an outpouring at the foot of the cross that surges from the heart of the Passover.

Matthew 26:2 states, "Passover begins in two days..." It was almost time for the Lamb of God to be the final sacrifice. The Message paraphrases the beginning of Galatians 4:4 this way: "But when the time arrived that was set by God the

Father, God sent His Son..." Just as that Scripture speaks of the perfect timing of His birth, Mathew 26:2 sets the impeccable precision of His final week. Leon Morris's commentary brings great insight here:

> The Passover was the great feast that commemorated the deliverance of the Israelites from Egypt. A central feature of the observance was the offering of a lamb or kid in sacrifice, and, after the ritual disposition of parts of the animal, the eating of the carcass in companies of ten or more in private homes. From early days the feast was joined with the Feast of Unleavened Bread; the combined observance lasted a week. All this made Passover an especially suitable time for Jesus to lay down His life for His people. The thought of a sacrifice leading to the freedom of the people of God from their slavery in Egypt was in the air at the time when the greater sacrifice that would set people free everywhere was to be offered.[3]

Not only was this a suitable time, it was the picture-perfect time. The sacrificial death of Jesus painted the flawless picture of what all other Passover celebrations had foreshadowed for over 1500 years. And it was almost time!

REFLECT: Consider what the early Jewish historian Josephus said about the "several hundred thousand lambs that were herded through the streets of Jerusalem every Passover." As you picture that scene in your mind, meditate on the final week of Jesus' earthly life as He makes His entry into Jerusalem. At the time of that Passover, no one probably saw Jesus as a lamb headed to slaughter. Looking back on that week, we are privileged to have Scripture that enlightens us to that spiritual truth.

RESPOND: How can you live your daily life in a way that continually expresses your thanks for the ultimate sacrifice Jesus paid for the penalty of your sins? Right now, it should be time for you to worship Him in spirit and in truth.

DAY 27

Preparation for the Passover

On the first day of the Festival of Unleavened Bread,
when the Passover lamb is sacrificed, Jesus' disciples
asked Him, "Where do you want us to go to prepare
the Passover meal for You?" So Jesus sent two of them
into Jerusalem with these instructions: "As you go into the
city, a man carrying a pitcher of water will meet you.
Follow him. At the house he enters, say to the owner,
'The Teacher asks: Where is the guest room where I can eat
the Passover meal with My disciples?' He will take you
upstairs to a large room that is already set up. That is where
you should prepare our meal." So the two disciples went
into the city and found everything just as Jesus had said,
and they prepared the Passover meal there.
Mark 14:12-16

"Jerusalem meant one thing for Jesus: certain death."
John Piper[1]

TODAY, I am reminded again of God's Word in Revelation 13:8: "... the Lamb who was slain from the creation of the world." Since before the beginning of time as we know it, God had been preparing for the ultimate Passover. From the time our world was created, God had begun preparation for Jesus, the Lamb of God, to be the final sacrifice for our sins. God did not save us on a last-minute whim. He loves us so much that this was His perfect plan all along.

Jesus required His people to go to great lengths to prepare for every Passover remembrance. These guidelines are outlined in Exodus 12:14-20. First, for seven days leading up to Passover, they could only eat unleavened bread. On the first day of the week, all yeast had to be removed from their houses. So the home had to be thoroughly cleaned of all leaven before Passover. Every cooking area had to be deep cleaned to ensure there was no contamination of leaven. In addition, all cooking utensils that would be used for Passover had to be carefully cleaned according to the procedures of Jewish law. This detailed preparation does not even include everything that had to be done precisely concerning the lamb for sacrifice. These are just a few examples of the exhaustive preparation that had to be made for Passover.

Passover has always been about preparation. God prepared His sacrificial Lamb before the foundation of the world. The people of the Jewish nation have always prepared for Passover and still do. The progression moves from Father God to His chosen people to every Christ-follower. God expects us to take time to prepare for His working in our lives.

One commentary on Exodus made this outstanding observation:

> God provided what God required: a substitute sacrifice to die for his people.
>
> There is an obvious progression here, with the lamb serving as a representative for larger and larger groups of people. At first, God provided one lamb for one person. Thus Abraham offered a ram in place of his son Isaac. Next, God provided one lamb for one household. This happened at the first Passover, when every family in the covenant community offered its own lamb to God. Then, God provided one sacrifice for the entire nation. On the Day of Atonement, a single animal atoned for the sins of all Israel. Finally, the day came when John the Baptist "saw Jesus coming toward Him and said, 'Look, the Lamb of God, who takes away the sin of the world!'" (John 1:29; cf. John 11:50–52). God was planning this all along: one Lamb to die for one world. By His grace He has provided a lamb, "the Lamb that was slain from the creation of the world" (Revelation 13:8).[2]

God thought of everything to pay our sin debt in His perfect preparation and profound progression of a final sacrifice of the Lamb of God.

REFLECT and RESPOND: May the words from the Christ-Centered Exposition Commentary center your focus on all that God has prepared and is preparing for you:

> Jesus is indeed this Passover Lamb, and He is in complete control of the events leading to His death. The cross did not

catch Him off guard. No, it was a divine appointment scheduled, as Peter would write, "before the foundation of the world" (1 Peter 1:20). Jesus knew down to the last detail what was happening, and He joyfully embraced it (Hebrew 12:2). Such confidence in God's will should inspire us to trust Him even when the road of life may be difficult, painful, even deadly. Our God is in control![3]

DAY 28

The Lamb's Arrival

It was now almost time for the Jewish Passover celebration, and many people from all over the country arrived in Jerusalem several days early so they could go through the purification ceremony before Passover began. They kept looking for Jesus, but as they stood around in the Temple, they said to each other, "What do you think? He won't come for Passover, will He?" Meanwhile, the leading priests and Pharisees had publicly ordered that anyone seeing Jesus must report it immediately so they could arrest Him.

John 11:55-57

"Death may be the King of terrors . . .
but Jesus is the King of kings!""
Dwight L. Moody[1]

PEOPLE from everywhere descended on Jerusalem during the week of the Passover celebration. Everyone arrived early so that proper preparations could be made to commemorate Passover according to Jewish law. Scripture tells us that everyone was looking for Jesus. God's Word also states that people were debating on whether Christ would dare show up at this Passover.

R. Kent Hughes explains the scene:

The Passover was coming, and back in Jerusalem, the very air was electric. There were tense conversations everywhere. Some were dangerously loud, others in careful tones. You could hear them on every hand. "Do you think He is really going to come?" "Have you seen those guards over at the temple? I've never seen so many there at one time!" "No, I don't think He'll chance it." "Well, I think He'll come."[2]

While they were debating whether Jesus would come, they had no idea what Luke would later write in his Gospel: "When the days drew near for Him to be taken up, He set His face to go to Jerusalem" (Luke 9:51 ESV). While they were discussing if Jesus would show His face, Jesus was so determined to be there that He had already set His face.

We never need to fear whether Jesus will show up. In fact, He is consistently present and always right on time. Rather than doubt if He will come, we should set our hearts on doing whatever it takes to get into His presence.

It reminds me of the most famous invitational hymn in the history of Christianity: "Just as I Am." What follows is my paraphrase of what Robert J. Morgan said was the story behind the song.

Charlotte Elliott of Brighton, England, was embittered at God because of her health and disability. She often thought, *If God loved me, He would not have treated me this way.* A Swiss minister, Dr. Cesar Malan, visited Charlotte on May 9, 1822, hoping to witness to her. The encounter did not go well at first, as Charlotte lost her temper so badly at dinner that it embarrassed her family. They left her alone with Dr. Malan.

As the conversation continued, Charlotte finally asked, "If I wanted to become a Christian and to share the peace and joy you possess, what would I do?"

Dr. Malan's response was, "You would give yourself to God just as you are now, with your fightings and fears, hates and loves, pride and shame."

Charlotte's reply was, "I would come to God just as I am? Is that right?"[3]

That day Charlotte came to God just as she was, and Jesus saved her. She also found a special verse from God in John 6:37: "… whoever comes to Me, I will never drive away."

It would be years later that Charlotte would pen the words to her great hymn. Her brother, Reverend Henry Elliot, was a minster who was trying to raise support for children of poor ministers. To help him raise funds, Charlotte wrote a poem and had it printed for sale. That poem became the hymn "Just as I Am." Charlotte died at age eighty-two with the legacy of writing over 150 hymns. The greatest of these was her first, "Just as I Am," that has impacted millions of lives.

The question is not, "Will Jesus come?" The issue is, will you come to Jesus as you are with full confidence that whoever comes to Him will never be cast out?

REFLECT: Reflect on the words from verse 1 of "Just as I Am":

> "Just as I am, without one plea,
> But that Thy blood was shed for me.
> And that Thou bidst me come to Thee.
> O Lamb of God, I come, I come."[4]

RESPOND: The Lamb of God will come! What do you need to do today to come to Him?

DAY 29

The Last Lamb

When the hour came, Jesus and His apostles reclined at the
table. And He said to them, "I have eagerly desired to eat this
Passover with you before I suffer. For I tell you, I will not eat
it again until it finds fulfillment in the kingdom of God."
After taking the cup, He gave thanks and said, "Take this and
divide it among you. For I tell you I will not drink again from
the fruit of the vine until the kingdom of God comes."
And He took bread, gave thanks and broke it, and gave it
to them, saying, "This is my body given for you; do this
in remembrance of me." In the same way, after the supper
He took the cup, saying, "This cup is the new covenant
in my blood, which is poured out for you."
Luke 22:14-20

"Jesus took the tree of death so you could have the tree of life."
Timothy Keller[1]

When Jesus reached the Upper Room with His disciples, they celebrated the age-old celebration of the Passover. However, this Passover would be a fulfillment of all previous Passovers. After this celebration, the disciples would always look at Passover in a different light. All the lambs that had been sacrificed would be fulfilled in one last sacrifice, that of Jesus Christ, the Passover Lamb. Jesus would be the final sacrifice, the ultimate fulfilment. He is the Last Lamb.

Jesus passed out the cup and said, "This cup is the new covenant in my blood, which is poured out for you." The word used for *new* in this text is *kainos*. The word means "new in quality" because "nothing exactly like this has ever been found before." A second word for *new* found in the New Testament is *neos*. This means "new in time." So while *neos* is defined as "more recent in time," *kainos* is translated as "different in nature from the old." This Passover meal would have a brand new significance with a nature distinct from all 1500 years of Passover celebrations. *Kainos* is the same word used in Revelation 21:5: "He who was seated on the throne said, 'I am making all things new!'" Because Jesus is the Last Lamb, the quality of things will be forever changed.

The ancient historian Josephus indicated that approximately 250,000 lambs were sacrificed each year[2] However, the blood shed for the staggering number of lambs sacrificed through the years couldn't come close to one drop of blood from the Lamb of God. Only His blood could purchase our redemption. It would take the blood of Jesus Christ to make all things new. John 6:53-58 records some very interesting words spoken by the Lamb of God:

> Jesus said to them, "Very truly I tell you, unless you eat the flesh of the Son of Man and drink his blood, you have no

life in you. Whoever eats My flesh and drinks My blood has eternal life, and I will raise them up at the last day. For My flesh is real food and My blood is real drink. Whoever eats My flesh and drinks My blood remains in Me, and I in them. Just as the living Father sent Me and I live because of the Father, so the one who feeds on Me will live because of Me. This is the bread that came down from heaven. Your ancestors ate manna and died, but whoever feeds on this bread will live forever."

Not only was the Lamb spotless, slaughtered, shared, a substitute, symbolic, and the source of our salvation, but only the Lamb satisfies. There is a feast on the table at Passover, and Jesus is the sacrificial Lamb. You must partake of Jesus personally. You must depend on Jesus as your bread of life and as your sacrificial Lamb. To experience a personal relationship with Jesus, you must feast on Him as the Lamb. A growing personal relationship with Jesus is the only thing that can satisfy the hunger and thirst of your soul. Have you found your true spiritual satisfaction in the Last Lamb?

REFLECT and RESPOND: Consider and respond to James Montgomery Boice's thoughts on this subject:

Is He as real to you spiritually as something you can taste or handle? Is He as much a part of you as that which you eat? Do not think me blasphemous when I say that He must be as real and as useful to you as a hamburger and french fries. I say this because, although He is obviously far more real and useful than these, the unfortunate thing is that for many people He is much less.[3]

DAY 30

The Final Sacrifice

It was the day of preparation, and the Jewish leaders didn't
want the bodies hanging there the next day, which was the
Sabbath (and a very special Sabbath, because it was Passover
week). So they asked Pilate to hasten their deaths
by ordering that their legs be broken.
Then their bodies could be taken down.
John 19:31

*"At the very center of the biblical faith of the biblical vision of
ultimate spiritual reality is the bloody death of a helpless victim."*
Timothy Keller[1]

I MUST BE honest and admit that sometimes I skip parentheses when I'm reading a book. Many times, parentheses are just asides or references, and the book makes sense even when you omit them. However, Scripture is an entirely different kind of book, written by the God of all Creation. There is nothing in His Word considered unimportant or unnecessary. In fact, it is the parenthesis that makes the Bible more easily understood. John 19:31 contains a parenthesis that is extremely beneficial. It reveals to us that the day after Jesus died was the Sabbath "(and a very special Sabbath, because it was Passover week.)"

The Sabbath that followed the day after Jesus' crucifixion was a *high Sabbath*, a Sabbath that coincided with one of seven annual festivals on the Jewish calendar: Passover, Feast of Unleavened Bread, Feast of Firstfruits, Pentecost, Feast of Trumpets, Day of Atonement, and the Feast of Tabernacles. This high Sabbath was for Passover.

These seven Sabbaths were also regular Sabbaths and therefore considered "double holy." In God's sovereignty, Jesus would be laid in the tomb just before the beginning of the day considered twice as holy as a regular Sabbath. In His perfect plan for redemption, God also ordained the Passover Sabbath for our Passover Lamb, something perfectly planned and spiritually significant.

It would be in the minds of all devout Jews not to do anything that would render them unclean and disqualify them for the celebration of the Passover high Sabbath. These Jewish leaders did not want the crucified bodies hanging overnight. They were obeying the Old Testament law of Deuteronomy 21:22-23:

If someone guilty of a capital offense is put to death and their body is exposed on a pole, you must not leave the body hanging on the pole overnight. Be sure to bury it that same day, because anyone who is hung on a pole is under God's curse. You must not desecrate the land the Lord your God is giving you as an inheritance.

It is amazing to me that these Jewish leaders didn't want to desecrate the land, but they had no problem crucifying our Lord. They had associated Jesus' death on the cross as God's curse, rather than realizing it was God's cure. Yet even in their hypocrisy, they were fulfilling the prophesy of God that declared Jesus' legs would not be broken. Psalm 34:20 says, "He protects all His bones, not one of them will be broken." Two separate times in John 19, God's Word clarifies that His bones were not broken (vv. 33, 36).

Even this significant detail points back to Jesus as our Passover Lamb. Exodus 12:46 and Numbers 9:12 both declare that none of the legs of the Passover lambs could be broken. Could it be that God specifically gave instructions 1500 years before Jesus would be crucified to show His precise plan to save the world through the death of His Son?

In addition to desecrating the land, touching a dead man rendered a person unclean for seven days (See Numbers 19:13). How ironic and misguided. The religious leaders did not want to miss the celebration of the Passover, so they rushed to kill God's Passover Lamb. These religious leaders missed the person who was the sole reason for the party. How do you celebrate the festival of Passover and miss the final sacrifice? May we never be so hypocritical in our religion that we miss the relationship with our Redeemer.

REFLECT: In what ways are the Priest and Levite in the parable of the Good Samaritan like the religious leaders mentioned in John 19? In what ways do we celebrate Christmas the same way the religious leaders celebrated the High Sabbath of Passover? How do we miss the holy moments on a day set aside to be twice as holy?

RESPOND: How can you live out your daily walk with Jesus without missing the Person of Jesus with whom you are supposed to be walking? Seek a relationship with Jesus over a routine about Jesus.

DAY 31

One More Reminder

Get rid of the old "yeast" by removing this wicked person from among you. Then you will be like a fresh batch of dough made without yeast, which is what you really are. Christ, our Passover Lamb, has been sacrificed for us.
1 Corinthians 5:7

"I want to stop writing, stare you in the face, and scream:
Jesus died!
He chose the most grueling death to bring you to God!
Everything is changed! You and I were destined for a horrifying
encounter with God—we were 'objects of wrath' (Ephesians 2:3)—
But that has all changed!"
Francis Chan[1]

WITH TEN DAYS left in our 41-day journey, let's look deeper at 1 Corinthians 5:7. We looked at this verse back on Day 7, and it is a key verse in our pursuit of spiritual victory. Today, we will focus more on a word study of a key verb as one more reminder of Christ, our Passover Lamb.

The word *sacrificed* is an interesting term on multiple levels. First, the meaning of this word sends a powerful message. The Greek word is *thyo*. *Thyo* means "to kill as a sacrifice and offer on an altar." Therefore, this word speaks both of a slaughtering and offering. There is a substantial difference between an animal just being put to death and something butchered in order to be offered. This word speaks of something that was slain as a sacrifice or a spiritual offering. *Thyo* is found fourteen times in the New Testament. It is translated once as "butchered," four times as "kill," and the other nine times as "a sacrifice for an offering."

God didn't just send His Son to die; He sent Him as a sacrifice. That's why He is called our Passover Lamb. Jesus was offered in our place. He wasn't just slain as a sin offering for all mankind; He took our place as our substitute. In reality, Christ was a double substitute. He died in fulfillment of all sacrificial lambs in history; in addition, He died in the place of sinners who deserved punishment.

Jesus was offered up at Golgotha, the place of the skull, so that we could find pardon that leads to a fulfilled life. Jesus was sacrificed between two thieves so we could be stolen away from Satan's grip. We should never forget God's offering or Christ's sacrifice. As the Jews rid their house of impurities before the Passover, we are free to live clean lives because of our Passover Lamb. He was the final sacrifice for our sins. He was the offering that provided the payment for the cost of redemption.

In addition to the meaning of the word *sacrifice*, the tense of the verb is another spiritual reminder. In 1 Corinthians 5:7, the action is found in aorist passive tense. Some scholars believe aorist is simply the past tense. However, renowned Greek scholar Bill Mounce makes the argument that the aorist tense is so much more than past tense: "... the aorist is so much more than 'past time,' and in fact time is significantly secondary to the real gist of the tense."[2]

The following is one example of how to view the aorist tense. You are in a helicopter flying over a parade. From that vantage point, you can see the whole parade. This is a different perspective from being in the parade and only seeing what is directly around you. In a way, aorist tense describes a more complete view of our past.

Therefore, "Christ our Passover Lamb has been sacrificed for us." In the past, Jesus died for us. As we look at the whole of what this means, it impacts every area of our everyday lives. The big picture is that Jesus was sacrificed as an offering so that we would have the opportunity to be transformed from the inside. And it is passive meaning, God the Father offered His only Son as the sacrifice. God sent Jesus to be our Passover Lamb.

REFLECT: Do you see the whole of what God did when Jesus became our Passover Lamb? Spend some time reflecting on what that truly means and why it is so important that Christ was slaughtered for the purpose of becoming an offering.

RESPOND: Read Romans 12:1. In view of God's mercy, how can you offer your body to Jesus Christ as a living sacrifice that is holy and pleasing to God? Are you serving God with true and proper worship?

DAY 32

The Shepherd's Voice

…but the Lord was not in the wind
…but the Lord was not in the earthquake
…but the Lord was not in the fire:
and after the fire a still small voice.
1 Kings 19:11-12 (KJV)

"If you do all the talking when you pray,
how will you ever hear God's answers?"
Aiden Wilson Tozer[1]

WE HAVE ALREADY WELL ESTABLISHED that some of the most familiar and well-loved passages of Scripture contain references to shepherds and sheep. The metaphor is clear:

GOD AS OUR SHEPHERD: God is wise, compassionate, tender, and protective as He guards and guides.

PEOPLE AS HIS SHEEP: People are dull, easily disoriented, and defenseless in the face of danger. People, like sheep, are wayward when left to their own. (Really, that's just polite talk. Sheep are dumb and people are, too).

However, the analogy goes deeper than just to draw from characteristics of ranchers and ewes. There is a beautiful relationship between shepherd and sheep that points us to the heart of God. The flock is His treasure.

God led His flock out of Egypt in the Exodus (Psalm 78:52). He regathers them from the Exile (Psalm 80:1-3). And He weeps over their waywardness as sheep without a shepherd (Matthew 9:36). The relationship of trust and obedience begins with the gentle, calming, wooing voice of the Shepherd.

God calls to us. He leads us with tender mercy and loving-kindness. When the Shepherd calls to the sheep, it is a reminder of His presence. His sheep know His voice and they follow.

The familiar lines of the 23rd Psalm give us indication of where it is that Jesus wants to guide us. His desire for you is green pastures, still waters, and an overflowing cup. He offers security, even in the presence of your enemies. All of this comes from His presence, dwelling in His house. But we must hear and heed His voice. We must submit to his rod and his staff. We must follow Him obediently. As the Good Shepherd leads, we must come after Him.

Obedience is a word that generally has a negative conno-

tation. To obey is often considered restrictive or even puni-
tive, but not so with the gentle voice of the Shepherd. Once I
heard His voice calling me out of my life of sinful rebellion, I
realized that obedience was liberating and that my misery
actually came from trying to live life apart from Jesus.

God's kindness leads us to repentance (Romans 2:4), and
His heart for us leads us to abundant life. Only Jesus, the
Great Shepherd, makes life make sense. He alone can lead
you to purpose and life. Pastor David Platt said, "The riches
of His kindness toward us are intended to lead us to run from
sin."[2] It is only with Christ as our Shepherd that life is really
worth living and we begin to live in the real sense of the
word. It is in trusting and obeying that we receive abundant
life.

REFLECT: Do you long to hear from God? Open His Word.
The Bible contains the Spirit-inspired, perfect words of God.
There, we find the promise of eternal life and the beautiful
voice of our Shepherd who leads us to spiritual maturity and
where we meet God Himself. Stand in awe and listen.

RESPOND: Do you long to hear from God? Open your heart.
Ask the Lord to speak to you. One of the best ways to
heighten your spiritual listening is to ask God to help. He
promises to answer when we call upon Him (Jeremiah 33:3 &
Psalm 91:15).

Father, I want to hear Your voice. Heighten my awareness of
Your leading. Empower me to put away busyness, distrac-
tion, and confusion. Like Samuel, I simply come before you
praying, "Speak, Lord; for your servant is listening." In Jesus'
Name, amen.

DAY 33

The Shepherd's Love

"I have revealed You to them, and I will continue to do so.
Then Your love for me will be in them, and I will be in them."
John 17:26

How deep the Father's love for us
How vast beyond all measure
That He should give His only Son
To make a wretch His treasure.[1]

I LOVE to give gifts at Christmastime. I fancy myself a good
gift giver. However, I bet if you talked to my family, they
might tell you that on occasion, my gifts have been quirky or
eccentric. But I try to find things that are unique and memo-
rable to the recipient. A few years ago, I gave my wife a set of
canvas photos of various places we've lived. They were very

random pictures that wouldn't mean anything significant to most others, but were a treasure to her and me.

God is the ultimate gift giver. Perhaps the most recognizable verse in all the Bible expresses this: "For God so loved the world that He gave..."[2] The priceless gift of the Son reflects the great love of the Father. If you want to see the true beauty and wonder of the love of God, peer into the manger in Bethlehem. Christmas demonstrates how deeply God loves. He gave His Son to be our Savior and our sacrifice.

Nowhere do we find a clearer picture of the love of God than in the sacrifice of Jesus. Not only did God give His Son, but He gave up His Son. John explains, "This is real love — not that we loved God, but that He loved us and sent His Son as a sacrifice to take away our sins" (1 John 4:10). Jesus gave His life on your behalf. God's wrath was appeased by the sacrifice of the sinless Lamb. Christ could not have sacrificed any more; He offered up His life. God's love for you is supreme, and supremely displayed in Jesus.

Hymn writer Frederick Martin Lehman, eloquently expressed the magnitude of the love of God:

> Could we with ink the ocean fill
> And were the skies of parchment made
> Were every stalk on earth a quill
> And every man a scribe by trade
> To write the love of God above
> Would drain the ocean dry
> Nor could the scroll contain the whole
> Though stretched from sky to sky.[3]

Oh, how great a love He has for us. In those moments when you don't feel loved, lovely, or loveable, stop and reflect on the settled fact that Jesus Christ, our Good Shepherd, loves you with an unending love. His love was demonstrated in His death, and His love for us reconciles us to God. "Nothing in all creation will ever be able to separate us from the love of God that is revealed in Christ Jesus our Lord" (Romans 8:39).

REFLECT: Consider these thoughts and Scriptures about the love of God:

- God's love is unfailing and unending. (Psalm 100:5)
- God pours His love into the hearts of believers. (Romans 5:5)
- As a Father, God loves by correcting His beloved children. (Proverbs 3:12)
- God's eternal plans are motivated by His love. (Ephesians 1:4-5)
- God preserves His people because of His great love. (Psalm 37:28)
- God's love is not based on our faithfulness, but rather, upon His. (Hosea 3:1)
- God demonstrated His love by sending His Son for sinners. (John 3:16)
- God demonstrated His love by the death of His Son for sinners. (Romans 5:8)
- God loves those who love and obey His Son. (John 14:21)
- As believers, we are to imitate God's universal love. (Matthew 5:44-45)
- God is love, and those who know God love others. (I John 4:7-8, 20-21)

RESPOND: Loving and gracious Heavenly Father, Your love is everlasting. Your love is overwhelming. You have loved me when I was not lovely or loveable. Your love has never failed, even when I have failed You. I am secure in the promise that nothing can ever separate me from Your love. I am grateful for Your sacrificial love that sent Christ to die on the cross. I love You, Lord. In Jesus' Name, amen.

DAY 34

The Shepherd's Heart

The hired hand runs away because he's working only for the money and doesn't really care about the sheep. "I am the good shepherd; I know my own sheep, and they know me, just as my Father knows me and I know the Father. So I sacrifice my life for the sheep.
John 10:13-15

Just when I need Him, Jesus is near,
Just when I falter, just when I fear;
Ready to help me, ready to cheer,
Just when I need Him most.[1]

IN 1986, Michael Morton was sentenced to life in prison for murdering his wife. He was released in 2011, twenty-five years after being convicted, when DNA testing proved he was not the killer. Morton describes an experience he had about fourteen years into his prison sentence. Morton's son, Eric, had stopped visiting him when Eric was twelve, and at eighteen, Eric wrote his father to tell him he had changed his last name. Can you imagine the intensity of such pain—falsely accused and now abandoned?

Morton said he was in absolute despair, in a deep depression, he cried out to God. There was no response for several weeks. Late one night, he recounts listening to a classical music station on the radio when a harp began to play. He said, "All of a sudden, in that dark prison cell in the middle of the night, I was bathed in this bright golden light. It was the weirdest, most unusual thing I've ever experienced in my life. I was warm, thrilled, ecstatic, calm, and at peace more than anything else. I felt this limitless compassion aimed right at me. It was like a mother's unconditional love magnified a million times—it was love. It was going to be okay—I knew it was the presence of God and now, life makes perfect sense." It would be eleven more years until he would be proven innocent, but Morton had an experience of the love of God that sustained him. Ponder again Morton's words, *"I knew, without a doubt, that this was the presence of God."*[2]

Michael Morton's story reminds me of Joseph from the Old Testament Book of Genesis. Joseph was betrayed, abandoned, and falsely imprisoned. We would probably give Joseph a pass for feeling sorry for himself. He had been done wrong, so he should be able to grovel a bit, right? Yet an amazing phrase marked the scenes of Joseph's story: "The Lord was with Joseph." We see it three times in Genesis 39[3] with a beautiful statement added in verse 21: "But the Lord was with Joseph in the prison and showed him his faithful love." The heart of God was revealed to Joseph by God's nearness. The faithfulness of God's love was revealed to Joseph by the presence of God. To Joseph, God was the Good Shepherd.

Few of us have faced that level of rejection and heartache (of Joseph's or of Michael Morton's), but any of us can experience that same peace and faithful love. The comforting presence of God, our Shepherd, brings hope from despair. Just as a shepherd moves toward a lost sheep in its helpless condition, the heart of God is drawn to our deep places of pain. The Psalmist extols, "The Lord is close to the brokenhearted; He rescues those whose spirits are crushed."[4]

God will not let go of us. He pursues and He remains. This loving shepherd is greater than our broken hearts. Who is the Good Shepherd? Jesus, the One who comes to make the invisible God visible and the unapproachable God accessible. Jesus, the God who ceaselessly comes to find us when we have lost our way or forgotten to Whom we belong.

REFLECT: How can I learn more of the heart of God?
By spending time in His Word. (John 5:39)
By learning more and more about Jesus. (1 Peter 3:18)
By spending time with the Lord in prayer. (James 4:8)

RESPOND: Dear Heavenly Father, You are our ever-present help in times of trouble. In times of despair and even doubt, You remain faithful and loving. Lord, open my eyes to see and enable my mind to grasp how deep and wide and long is Your love for me. Thank You for Your loving heart, O, Shepherd Who watches over me. In Jesus' Name, amen.

DAY 35

The Shepherd's Path

He makes me lie down in green pastures,
He leads me beside quiet waters.
Psalm 23:2 (NIV)

Savior, like a shepherd lead us,
Much we need Thy tender care;
In Thy pleasant pastures feed us,
For our use Thy folds prepare.[1]

GOD KNOWS EXACTLY what we need, when we need it, and before we ever know it. And God supplies all our needs. He is the wise, all-knowing Shepherd who leads us down right paths. If those things are all true (and they are), it seems everyone would follow this Shepherd (but they don't). So why would we struggle so much against His leading? Why is it so much easier to do everything else but God's will? It seems so obvious that we should trust and obey Him. After all, He loves us, He knows and wants the best for us, and He leads us in the right paths.

But we are sheep. And following is not always easy for us. Sheep are hesitant to move toward the dark or into an enclosed area. Sheep are easily spooked and anxious. And often, we (like sheep) think we know which path is best.

In Psalm 23, David wrote of the paths down which God leads as he acknowledges the Lord's leadership in his own life. Psalm 23 has been dubbed "The Shepherd's Psalm," and David writes from his own shepherding experiences as well as from his loving relationship with his Good Shepherd. Consider where the Shepherd's path sometimes leads:

- The Good Shepherd leads us down a path to a place of rest.
- The Good Shepherd leads us down a path to a place of provision and peace.
- The Good Shepherd leads us down a path right into the presence of our enemies. That seems to be a place we'd want to avoid, yet the Good Shepherd leads us there with confidence and courage.
- The Good Shepherd leads us down a path of righteousness.
- The Good Shepherd leads us down a path to eternal joy.

If you are a believer, you can trust the Lord to guide you down the right path. Even when the pathway is dark, even when it seems ominous and frightening, He is with you all the way, guiding, leading, and nurturing. Trust Him. His path is best.

When it came to the path of redemption for all of mankind, God knew best, as well. Songwriter and composer Geron Davis penned powerful words about God's clear understanding of what redemption would require in the song "It Took A Lamb":

> *He could've Come in all His splendor.*
> *Greater than the eye has ever seen.*
> *He could've come in robes of scarlet.*
> *And all the world, would see that He is king.*

> *He could've ridden on a White Horse*
> *As a warrior and conquered every land.*
> *But He knew that if redemption's price were paid,*
> *It would take a Lamb.*[2]

When we have a heavenly Shepherd who supplies all our needs, how foolish to seek out the stagnant pools and broken cisterns this world supplies. When the Good Shepherd leads us down the paths of His choosing, why would we wander into unknown places of heartache and grief? When the sinless, spotless Lamb of God is all-sufficient for our redemption, why would we toil at trying to impress God with our fleshly works?

RELAX. Trust the Good Shepherd.

LISTEN. Hear His gentle voice beckoning you on.

FOLLOW. In simple obedience, stay close to the One Who is calling.

ENJOY. Live in the freedom that comes under His protective care.

REFLECT: Have you ever had a coach, teacher, mentor, friend, etc., that you looked up to as a role model? What about that person made you want to follow in his or her footsteps? What hesitation do you have about following Jesus? Do you see following the path of God as frightening or freeing? What challenges do we face if we follow Jesus as our shepherd?

RESPOND: Dear Heavenly Father, Thank You for leading me and guiding me in the path of Your choosing. I worship You because of Your boundless knowledge. Your ways are not my ways; Your ways are best. Keep me from straying from Your path of righteousness and remind me, day by day, that Your path is always for my good and for Your glory. In Jesus' Name, amen.

DAY 36

T he Shepherd's Promise

"...And be sure of this: I am with you always,
even to the end of the age."
Matthew 28:20

"Safety comes in our nearness to God,
not in our distance from our enemies."
Dillon Burroughs[1]

FEAR. Anxiety. Uncertainty. Unrest—apt descriptors of life for
many over the past few years. A global pandemic, political
upheaval, racial division, and financial instability have
chipped away at our collective psyche. Empty store shelves,
broken supply chains, and skyrocketing prices have
disrupted the normal rhythm and flow of our lives. Many
things long considered to be a given are now points of uncer-

tainty. In your lifetime, could you ever consider *food insecurity* to be a thing? Few in the Western world could. Foreign policy professor Elise Labott describes this growing global angst:

> People in fragile states, already suffering from diminished trust in their government, have felt further abandoned as they face disruptions in public services, rising food prices, and massive economic hardships, such as unemployment and reduced wages.[2]

It's no surprise that crises are looming and people are more fragile and vulnerable than ever. Spooked sheep scatter. People are scrambling to make sense of the world, and they are running in fear. Sheep without a shepherd move about aimlessly. Left to their own, they wandering here and there. They are often oblivious to the dangers around them.

But we *do* have a Shepherd. We are under the nurturing care of One who is near to us. God makes an eternal promise that He will be with us; He will never leave or forsake us. This powerful promise of Christ's presence brings comfort, confidence, and courage. Time and again, God assured His people with His presence, just as a shepherd's presence would bring reassurance to a physical flock.We read of God's promise of nearness throughout Scripture.

- To Jacob (Genesis 28:15)
- To Joshua and the people of God (Deuteronomy 31:8; Joshua 1:5, 9)
- As a comforting Guide (Psalm 73:23-26)
- To Solomon (1 Chronicles 28:20)
- For the poor and needy (Isaiah 41:10-17)
- To all believers (Matthew 28:20)

That promise was vividly actualized in the arrival of Jesus Christ in Bethlehem—God incarnate; deity cloaked in human flesh; Emmanuel, God with us. Jesus, the Messiah, was and is the express image of God.

Seventeenth-century Baptist Pastor Benjamin Keach eloquently described the beautiful gift of nearness that Jesus' arrival afforded:

> We may from hence perceive the wonderful love, goodness, and condescension of God to mankind, Who seeing how unable we are to understand, comprehend, conceive, or take in the knowledge of himself, (Who is so infinite and inaccessible in His Being, Glory, And Majesty) is pleased to stoop so low, as to afford us a figure, image, and lively representation of Himself, that so we might not frame false ideas of God, or entertain any vain or unworthy apprehensions of Him in our minds.[3]

We can rest in our Shepherd. We can experience the love and goodness of God by following Jesus Christ. Resting in Him means that we look to and trust in His presence. We pay attention to the Shepherd. We walk in an awareness of His nearness. He has promised to be an ever-present help, but we often wander. Fix your gaze upon Christ! Pay attention; make room. When we walk in the presence of God, the busiest moment of the day is no different from the still, quiet prayer closet. Even in the midst of chaos and clutter, noise, and nuisance, your soul can be stilled in the serenity of His presence.

In this Advent season, other voices clamor for your attention, and you might find it difficult to maintain focus on God. Simply turn back toward Him now. Look to the Good

Shepherd, Who promised to be with you to the end of the age.

REFLECT: Are you struggling with anxiety, pressure, or uncertainty in these chaotic days? To whom are you running? Who or what is your refuge? If you are looking to anyone or anything other than Christ for solace, it will be short-lived. Repent and turn to Emmanuel, God with us.

RESPOND: Dear Heavenly Father, I ask for your forgiveness in all the ways I've wandered so far from Your presence. In these troubling days, we need your healing and grace. Thank you for reminding us You are always faithful and that You're constantly at work on behalf of your children—powerfully, completely, drawing us closer to you again. Help us to live aware, to choose wisely, and to stay close to you, anchored in your truth. In Jesus' Name, amen.

DAY 37

orthy

Then I saw a Lamb that looked as if it had been slaughtered,
but it was now standing between the throne and the four
living beings and among the twenty-four elders… And they
sang a new song with these words: "You are worthy to take
the scroll and break its seals and open it. For you were
slaughtered, and your blood has ransomed people for
God from every tribe and language and people and
nation. And you have caused them to become a Kingdom of
priests for our God. And they will reign on the earth."
Revelation 5:6-10

*"The privilege of praise is ours now. We can sing of the Lamb of
God's worth every day through our attitudes, words, and actions."*
Denise Loock[1]

As we march closer and closer to Christmas Day, I hope you have invested thought in God's marvelous metaphors of shepherd and sheep. I hope you have come to recognize the wisdom and care that God displays in His Word, drawing from this analogy. He is the Good Shepherd, tender and compassionate. We are the sheep, defenseless and dependent.

Now, let's turn our attention again to Jesus, the Lamb. The purpose of the Bible is to reveal God's plan of redemption to fallen mankind. And that redemption demanded the wage of sin: DEATH. We know the gift of God's Son was not completed in His Nativity but in His sacrifice. Jesus was born to die. Blood sacrifice was required. Our redemption's price would take a lamb. This seems extreme but only when we minimize the depth of our sin.

The Holy Living God is serious about sin. God's first act outside of creation was to cover Adam and Eve with a garment procured from sacrifice.[2] God chose to use a blood sacrifice as part of the system implemented for worship by the Jewish people. Each time blood was shed, it reminded the people of life and death, of relationship and separation. The sacrifice of a lamb reminded the people of God's deliverance in Egypt and the demand for total obedience. The cost of the sacrificed animal represented a price that had to be paid by the one providing the offering. Each time a blood sacrifice was made, the one giving it was reminded of the cost of sin. The wilderness tabernacle carried this theme forward. The bloodstained story of redemption systematically unfolds in Scripture in what famed pastor W. A. Criswell dubbed, the "Scarlet Thread of the Bible," culminating in the final, sufficient sacrifice of Jesus Christ, the perfect Lamb of God.[3]

Christ's death demonstrated God's complete love for us. The slain Lamb was the only means to save us from the sin that separated us from the presence of God. It is through His death on the cross as God's perfect sacrifice for sin and His resurrection that we can now have eternal life. God Himself has provided the offering that atones for our sin. Oh, what a Savior!

Fast forward to the heavenly vision John was given, recorded for us in the Book of Revelation. I would imagine John expected to see a Lion, but what he saw was a Lamb with the marks of death still upon him. This is vitally important. Yes, Jesus is the King of Kings and the Lord of Lords. Yes, Jesus is the Lion of the Tribe of Judah. But His identity as the slain Lamb of God marked by the scars of redemption's price evokes praise and worship and laud and honor. Worthy is the Lamb! Those marks of death are still upon the Lamb and will be for all eternity.

The Lion of Judah and the Lamb that was slain unites two themes that run throughout the Bible. Lions represent majesty, power, rule and authority. Lambs represent gentleness, purity, and sacrifice. Lions conquer; lambs submit. Lions roar; lambs die. Jesus is the ultimate embodiment of both as He is the One who conquers by submitting and is worthy of all praise. The song of those around the throne reverberates praise for the price of ransom. Jesus, the slain Lamb Who now lives has purchased redemption by His blood. Worthy is the Lamb!

At Christmas time, we often sing the chorus, "Oh, come let us adore Him."[4] This Christmas, recognize Him as more than a babe in a manger. Acknowledge Him as the Lamb Who was slain before the foundation of the world. He is the sacrifice for our salvation. He is the One Who overcame death and grave. Worthy is the Lamb!

REFLECT: Ponder the magnitude of Christ on the cross. What does it mean for us that Jesus is the Lamb of God? List out some of the ramifications (Ex. Our sin-debt is paid, we are reconciled, we are cleansed…)

RESPOND: Dear Jesus, Our precious Lamb of God, Thank You for taking my place, for dying the death my sins deserve and for paying the price my sins demand. Thank You that I can go straight to God in prayer. You bridged the gap and made a way for us. Jesus, You have torn the curtain of separation. Because of Your death, I can come before God in confidence and trust. Your blood has made me clean. Thank you, Jesus! You alone are worthy! In Jesus' Name, amen.

DAY 38

B lessing and Honor

Then I looked again, and I heard the voices of thousands and
millions of angels around the throne and of the living beings
and the elders. And they sang in a mighty chorus:
"Worthy is the Lamb who was slaughtered—to receive power
and riches and wisdom and strength and honor and glory
and blessing." And then I heard every creature in heaven and
on earth and under the earth and in the sea.
They sang: "Blessing and honor and glory and power
belong to the one sitting on the throne and to the Lamb
forever and ever." And the four living beings said, "Amen!"
And the twenty-four elders fell down
and worshiped the Lamb.
Revelation 5:11-14

"Once in our world, a stable had something in it that was bigger than our whole world."
C.S. Lewis[1]

I ALWAYS FEEL a bit nostalgic at Christmas. I think back to my childhood to the decorations our family treasured and proudly displayed year after year. I dream of the amazing smells that wafted from my mom's kitchen as she cooked and baked. It only takes a few notes of a familiar Christmas song to transport me back to a simple time of life when Christmas was about so many of these wonderful things. Christmas is a time for giving and receiving. It is wonderful time to invest in family and friends. It is a time to celebrate and a time to remember. And Christmas is a beautiful time for worship. Why? Because Christmas is about God's redeeming love for mankind and our rescue from utter disaster by the work of Jesus, the Lamb.

In Revelation 5, we're given a glimpse into worship occurring around God's throne in heaven—rapturous worship ascribing blessing, honor, praise, and worth to Jesus Christ. And every created being is part of this choir. They worship the Lamb because of His death and in the presence of His resurrected life.

The heavenly choir proclaims Jesus is worthy of worship because of His death and the redemption that it purchased. We've said repeatedly that for redemption's price to be paid, it would take a sinless, spotless lamb... and Jesus is that lamb. Hallelujah!

Worship becomes central to our Christmas experience. We look back in reflection. We look around in celebration. We look forward in hope, and we look up in praise and adoration. While there's nothing wrong with singing about sleigh rides and snow or about roasted chestnuts or coming home for Christmas, the song of the slain Savior marks the hope of this holy day. Christmas is a time for worship because Jesus is our sacrificial Lamb. Let me encourage you to be mindful of the gospel that is implanted in so many of our beloved Christmas carols.

> Mild He lays His glory by, Born that man no
> more may die.
> Born to raise the sons of earth, Born to give
> them second birth.[2]

> No more let sins and sorrows grow, Nor thorns
> infest the ground;
> He comes to make His blessings flow Far as the
> curse is found.[3]

> Nails, spear shall pierce Him through, The cross
> be borne for me, for you.
> Hail, hail the Word made flesh, The Babe, the
> Son of Mary.[4]

These songs reflect the anthem of praise and worship John saw around heaven's throne. And Jesus, the Lamb of God, is in the middle of it all.

John Stott emphasizes the centrality of Jesus, the Lamb, in his book, *The Cross of Christ*:

One cannot fail to notice, or to be impressed by, the seer's repeated and uninhibited coupling of 'God and the Lamb. The person he places on an equality with God is the Savior who died for sinners. He depicts him as mediating God's salvation, sharing God's throne, receiving God's worship (the worship due to him) and diffusing God's light. And his worthiness, which qualifies him for these unique privileges, is due to the fact that he was slain, and by his death procured our salvation.[5]

Jesus is worthy. He is worthy of praise and obedience. He is worthy of blessing and honor. Worship Him today. Don't miss the gospel this Christmas. Worship Him for His grace and His redeeming love. As earth's perfect king, Jesus deserves honor and reverence from His loyal subjects. The glory of His holiness covers the earth. Every created being will one day bless His holy name. All of heaven worships Jesus as the Lamb that was slain. Let's make sure we do, too.

REFLECT: If Christ, the Lamb of God, is worthy of our worship, He is also worthy of our obedience. Are there activities or attitudes in your life that are not in keeping with our holy, loving God? Confess and forsake them today.

RESPOND: Dear Heavenly Father, my heart is filled with adoration as I consider the vastness of Your grace, mercy, and love. The depths to which Christ has gone to secure our redemption is overwhelming. I lift my eyes to You, the Lord of all creation, the Lord of our salvation, the soon and coming King. I worship You, Lord Jesus, for You alone are worthy. You are worthy to receive blessing and honor and glory and power forever. Amen.

DAY 39

Glory and Power

After this I saw a vast crowd, too great to count, from every
nation and tribe and people and language, standing in front
of the throne and before the Lamb. They were clothed in
white robes and held palm branches in their hands. And they
were shouting with a great roar, "Salvation comes from our
God who sits on the throne and from the Lamb!"
Revelation 7:9-10

It is about the greatness of God, not the significance of man.
God made man small and the universe big
to say something about himself.
John Piper[1]

MODERN TECHNOLOGY HAS MADE the world seem closer, if not smaller. With the advent of the internet, news travels farther and faster than ever. If someone famous sneezes on another continent, we can know it before they reach for a tissue. We have tools of connection that draw people together. Scientists have long talked about "chains" or "degrees of separation" between people all over the earth.[2] Our world, at times, does indeed seem small.

But this illusion says something about the human heart. We tend toward a distorted perspective of our importance and size, especially in light of the enormity of God. We don't have a sense of appropriate smallness. Some time ago, I read an article by Tom Ruprecht entitled, "It's Actually Not a Small World" that he wrote for *McSweeney's*. Included in the piece were the following quips about relationships and encounters:

Last Wednesday Alden Provost was in the United terminal at O'Hare. At the same time Justin Stangel, Alden's childhood friend, was in the Continental terminal. The two grew up next door to each other, but hadn't seen one another since Justin's family moved away twenty years before. 180,000 people pass through O'Hare every day and the United and Continental terminals are located quite a ways away from each other, so Alden and Justin didn't even come close to bumping into each another.

Last May 19th Chris Albers went to the Cloverleaf Mall, in Medford, Oregon, and parked in space 219. Amazingly, at the very same moment in the Cloverleaf Mall, in Duluth, Minnesota, a man also named Chris Albers parked in space

219. The only one aware of this odd coincidence, however, was God.[3]

These anecdotes help us to appreciate how big the world really is, but at the same time, they reveal how small we are in it. So, too, does the Bible. Revelation 7 is a stirring scene of future worship around God's throne. An innumerable crowd, comprised of people from every tribe, tongue, nation, and language is gathered around the throne to worship the Lamb of God. With a unified, roaring shout, they proclaim the glory and majesty and power of God, Who is the source of salvation. In purity and in joy, they ascribe worth to the worthy One.

We toss around the theological term *omnipotent* to describe God's divine power but can scarcely can take in the colossal magnitude of His capacity. God's power to create with only His spoken word is awe inspiring. His ability to rule over and sustain all things is mind boggling. Both the intricacies of the created order and the vastness of the universe is mesmerizing. The Old Testament prophet Isaiah raises the question, "Who else has held the oceans in his hand? Who has measured off the heavens with his fingers? Who else knows the weight of the earth or has weighed the mountains and hills on a scale?"[4] Yet these acts of creation and sustenance pale in comparison to the greatest demonstration of His power. God displayed the full magnitude of His omnipotence when He accomplished His redemptive work through Christ. His divine power secures our salvation for all eternity. He is the Lamb from Whom salvation comes, magnificent in glory and majestic in power.

REFLECT: Do you see God's glory being reflected through your life? If so, how? If not, then ask why. God desires to reflect His nature, His glory, and His power through every believer. God has promised to reflect His glory through those who walk in obedience to His commands.

RESPOND: Dear Heavenly Father, My heart is filled with adoration as I consider the vastness of Your grace, mercy, and love. The depths to which Christ has gone to secure our redemption is overwhelming. I lift my eyes to You, the Lord of all creation, the Lord of our salvation, the soon and coming King. I worship You, Lord Jesus, for You alone are worthy. You are worthy to receive blessing and honor and glory and power forever. Amen.

DAY 40

The Lamb's Book of Life

Nothing evil will be allowed to enter, nor anyone who practices shameful idolatry and dishonesty—but only those whose names are written in the Lamb's Book of Life.
Revelation 21:27

YOU'RE INVITED

Invitations like the fictitious one on the previous page are commonplace this time of year. Your mailbox or inbox may contain invitations requiring a response. You check the calendar for conflicts and R.S.V.P. with your intentions. Your prompt response is polite, so planning ahead is important.

We spend much of the Christmas season planning ahead, or, as I like to call it, "the state of getting ready." We have to get the house ready with decorations and tidy up for guests. We have to get the grocery lists ready, and once we have all the right ingredients, we have to get the food ready. We get the kids ready for pictures and pageants and parties, and then we get them ready for bed on Christmas Eve. We get the tree ready, the camera ready, the gifts ready, and on and on. Lots of getting ready goes into Christmas.

The people of Israel had been readying themselves for the arrival of Messiah for centuries. Approximately 700 years prior to the birth of Christ, there was a prophet named Isaiah who told the people of God what he saw concerning their future. What was in their future? The arrival of a child, their Savior. The dawning of light shattering deep darkness. Their Mighty God would become their Prince of Peace. Their Messiah would come and rule and reign eternally.

I hope by now that all of your getting ready is complete. It's Christmas Eve, after all. Maybe you have a few last minute details to wrap up, but by now, most everything should be set. But what about your spiritual readiness? Surely if you've journeyed this far with us, you've considered the significance of receiving the sacrifice of the Lamb. Jesus' substitutionary death paid the wage of sin, but it must be applied to your account for you to get credit. He graciously offers salvation full and free to those who believe. This offer is pure grace, undeserved and unmerited. The means by which you receive it is pure faith, trusting in His Word that the sacrifice of the Lamb is sufficient.

Why this talk about getting ready and making reservations? Seven times, the Book of Revelation references the Book of Life and twice mentions that the book belongs to the Lamb. Those whose names are written there belong to God. Scripture is clear that the only way to have eternal life is through the Lamb, and these people have attained it.

The Book of Life is a respondent list of sorts. The life and ministry of Christ—His arrival, His sinless life, His substitutionary death, and His victorious resurrection—came with an invitation. Romans 10:13 says, "For everyone who calls on the name of the Lord will be saved."[1] Calling upon His name is the R.S.V.P. When you call upon the name of Jesus for salvation, you are responding to His invitation. God extends an invitation for us to enter heaven through the Lamb.

FIT FOR HEAVEN

"Away in a Manger," one of the most beloved and well-known Christmas carols, was composed in the 1800s by William J. Kirkpatrick and James Ramsey Murray. The carol ends with an impassioned petition, a prayer of anticipation for heaven:

> Be near me Lord Jesus
> I ask you to stay
> Close by me forever,
> And love me, I pray.
> Bless all the dear children
> In thy tender care,
> And **fit us for heaven**
> To live with thee there. [2]

Faith in Jesus, the Lamb of God, is the only way we'll be fitted for heaven. Nothing impure or evil will enter that place, and the only way to be cleansed is the precious blood of the Lamb. We must respond to the invitation. Our names must be written in the Lamb's Book.

REFLECT: Do you know for certain that you have eternal life and that you will go to heaven when you die? If not, you can explore this more at 41series.com/newlife. If you're already a believer, spend time today thanking Jesus for being the sinless, spotless Lamb. He bought you with His blood, He cleanses you by His righteousness, and He keeps you by His power.

RESPOND: Luke 10:20 tells us, "But don't rejoice because evil spirits obey you; rejoice because your names are registered in heaven." Getting ready for heaven is not just making a reservation. We are to develop the values of the Kingdom right here on earth. Pray as Jesus prayed in Matthew 6, "Your Kingdom come, Your will be done, on earth as it is in heaven." Seek to do the will of God in the here and now and celebrate that you have made preparation for the by and by.
God sent His Son, Jesus of Nazareth, in the form of a man to remove the sin which separated mankind's heart from the heart of God. By entering the world as a man, God was able to take the sins of the entire world upon His own shoulders and pay the penalty of this separation by allowing His Son, Jesus Christ, to be separated from Him for a moment of time.

DAY 41

Cradle, A Cross, and a Crown

For you know that God paid a ransom to save you from the empty life you inherited from your ancestors. And it was not paid with mere gold or silver, which lose their value. It was the precious blood of Christ, the sinless, spotless Lamb of God.
1 Peter 1:18-19

"Now I can go into the Holy of Holies. I can kneel and make my petition known. I can go into the Holy of Holies, although I'm just a common man, because of God's redemption plan. I can boldly approach the throne."
Geron Davis[1]

MERRY CHRISTMAS! And thank you for walking this 41-day Christmas journey with us. We pray it has been a blessing of encouragement and refreshment as you've drawn near to Jesus Christ, the Lamb of God.

We've mentioned before the significance of the number *forty-one* as a symbol of victory. The number *forty* shows up often in the Bible, commonly in contexts dealing with judgment or testing. *Forty-one* often represents victory or an end to the trial or testing. These forty-one days of Advent readings culminate today (ON CHRISTMAS DAY), representing victory as we celebrate the glorious arrival of Jesus Christ, the Messiah.

The people of God endured a season of darkness and testing. Hearts grew heavy with longing and anticipation as they waited for deliverance. Christ's birth marked the end of that darkness. When Christ was born in Bethlehem, everything changed. Hope had come. But the Nativity was only one scene in the storyline. The good news of Christmas rests in the completed story, which included the cross of Calvary and beyond. We know the rest of the story. We are aware that Jesus moved from the cradle toward the cross. And we know that, even now, the story is not fully complete. We live between two worlds of His first advent and His return. We live in the Kingdom that is already, but not yet. Christ has come and has promised to come again.

Heaven awaits those whose names are in the Lamb's Book of Life, and their hope is anchored in His sure and steady promises. On this Christmas Day, ponder anew the scenes of redemption in the life of Jesus.

Scene One: The Cradle

Take a few moments to read the account of the birth of Jesus from Luke 2. Savor the story and slowly walk through the atmosphere of inexpressible joy, of peace made possible, of salvation seen.

Yes, we know the full story, but the participants in this scene did not. They weren't aware of a coming cross. They weren't thinking about a suffering savior. But we know that without this cradle of Christmas, there would be no cross of Calvary.

Consider the purpose of the coming of Jesus, the Lamb: "For I have come down from heaven to do the will of God who sent me, not to do my own will."[2]

Scene Two: The Cross

Take a few moments to read the account of the death of Jesus from Matthew 27. Savor the story and slowly walk through the atmosphere of excruciating pain, shame and mocking ridicule, and of that sacred head now wounded.

Jesus lived a sinless life. Because of this life, He was the only sufficient substitute for our sin. He willingly gave His life. Pastor Mark Jones contends, "If we do not understand Christ's death as voluntary, then we do not understand His death."[3] Christ's willingness to go to the cross demonstrates the depth of His love for the Father and for mankind. Jesus was not a helpless victim, torn between the will of God and sinful men, but a willing sacrifice who chose to lay down His life for the salvation of others. Christ, the sinless One, hung on the cross as all our sins were placed on Him, and He died in our place. Without the cross, we would have no hope of eternal life because of our sins. But upon the cross, the Lamb of God became sin in order that we might become the righteousness of God (2 Corinthians 5:21).

Scene Three: The Crown

Consider 1 Peter 1:3-4: "It is by his great mercy that we have been born again, because God raised Jesus Christ from the dead. Now we live with great expectation, and we have a priceless inheritance—an inheritance that is kept in heaven for you, pure and undefiled, beyond the reach of change and decay."

During Advent, you have prepared your hearts for the celebration of Christ's birth, so now let us challenge you to prepare your heart in the anticipation of His Return. A glorious future awaits. The best is yet to come!

REFLECT: Consider each scene of this redemptive story. Praise God for each scene and the significance that it brings to bear upon your redemption.
The cradle speaks of humility, as Christ emptied Himself. *For us, it brings the promise of peace with God.*
The cross speaks of humiliation, as Christ endured the scorn. *For us, it satisfied the perfect justice of the Father.*
The crown speaks of honor, as His Kingdom is eternally established. *For us, it brings hope (confident expectation) of all He has promised.*

RESPOND: Dear Heavenly Father, We thank You on this Christmas Day for the greatest gift ever given, the Lord Jesus Christ. Thank You that in Your wisdom, You knew redemption would require a Lamb. Thank You that in Your love and mercy, You provided us that Lamb. Thank You that You graciously extend salvation and that we receive it by faith. Thank You for the cradle; for the cross; and, hallelujah, thank You for the crown that is to come!

ALSO IN THE 41 SERIES

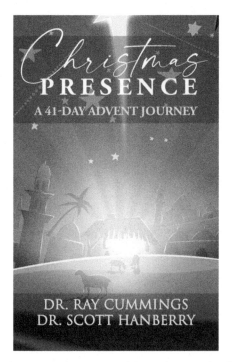

Advent is a season of expectant waiting and preparation for both the celebration of the Nativity of Christ at Christmas and the return of Christ at the Second Coming. It traditionally encompasses the four Sundays leading up to Christmas and is centered around the four themes of hope, peace, love, and joy. Christmas Presence will help you and your family prepare your hearts for the celebration of Christ's Nativity and the anticipation of His Return! For more information, visit www. 41series.com.

ALSO IN THE 41 SERIES

Would a guided devotional help you prepare for the most significant day on the Christian calendar, Easter Sunday? The authors of Christmas Presence: A 41-Day Advent Journey *offer a 41-day journey of walking with the God of resurrection power,* Raised to Walk: A 41-Day Easter Journey. *For more information, visit www.41series.com.*

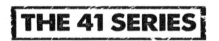

NOTES

Introduction

1. Davis, G. (n.d.). It Took a Lamb - lyrics and music by Geron and Becky Davis arranged by Gregbomia. Smule. Retrieved July 21, 2022, from https://www. smule.com/song/geron-and-becky-davis-it-took-a-lamb-karaoke-lyrics/ 461647045_399239/arrangement.

Day 1

1. Tozer, A. W. (n.d.). *48+ Promising Lamb Of God Quotes That Will Unlock Your True Potential.* Retrieved July 6, 2022, from https://quotlr.com/quotes-about-lamb-of-god.
2. Fink, J. (2019, December 25). *Why is it called Christmas? The origin and meaning of the name explained. Newsweek.*
3. Revelation 13:8 (NLT).
4. Davis, G. (n.d.). *It took a lamb - lyrics and music by Geron and Becky Davis arranged by Gregbomia.* Smule. Retrieved July 21, 2022, from https://www. smule.com/song/geron-and-becky-davis-it-took-a-lamb-karaoke-lyrics/ 461647045_399239/arrangement.

Day 2

1. Spurgeon, C. H. (1970, April 18). *Christ our Passover by C. H. Spurgeon.* Blue Letter Bible. Retrieved July 6, 2022, from https://www.blueletterbible. org/Comm/spurgeon_charles/sermons/0054.cfm.
2. Philip Graham Ryken and R. Kent Hughes, *Exodus: Saved for God's Glory.* (Wheaton, IL: Crossway Books, 2005), 328.

Day 3

1. Claiborne, S. (n.d.). *The most delighting Shane Claiborne quotes that are free to learn and Impress Others.* Retrieved July 6, 2022, from https://quotlr.com/ author/shane-claiborne.

Day 4

1. Edward Rowell, ed., *1001 Quotes, Illustrations, and Humorous Stories: For Preachers, Teachers, and Writers.* (Baker Publishing Group, 2008), 51.
2. Mark Cahill, *One Thing You Can't Do In Heaven.* (Rockwall, Texas: Biblical Discipleship Publishers, 2002), 34.
3. Ibid., 62.

Day 5

1. Philip Graham Ryken and R. Kent Hughes, *Exodus: Saved for God's Glory.* (Wheaton, IL: Crossway Books, 2005), 332.
2. Raymond C. Ortlund Jr. and R. Kent Hughes, *Isaiah: God Saves Sinners*, Preaching the Word (Wheaton, IL: Crossway Books, 2005), 356–357.
3. Ryken and Hughes, 333.

Day 6

1. Tim Chester, *Exodus for You*, ed. Carl Laferton, God's Word for You. (The Good Book Company, 2016), 88.
2. Jonathan Edwards, *A History of the Work of Redemption*, ed. John F. Wilson, *The Works of Jonathan Edwards*, 9 (New Haven, CT: Yale University Press, 1989), n.p.
3. Philip Graham Ryken and R. Kent Hughes, *Exodus: Saved for God's Glory* (Wheaton, IL: Crossway Books, 2005), 330.
4. Ibid., 330–331.

Day 7

1. Luther, Martin (n.d.). *48+ promising lamb of God quotes that will unlock your true potential*. Retrieved July 6, 2022, from https://quotlr.com/quotes-about-lamb-of-God.
2. Tom Wright, *Paul for Everyone: 1 Corinthians* (London: Society for Promoting Christian Knowledge, 2004), 59–60.

Day 8

1. Lucado, M. (2019, December 1). *18 amazing quotes about God's protection*. ChristianQuotes.info. Retrieved July 9, 2022, from https://www.

christianquotes.info/top-quotes/18-amazing-quotes-about-Gods-protection/.

Day 9

1. Yancy, Phillip. (2019, December 1). *18 amazing quotes about God's protection.* ChristianQuotes.info. Retrieved July 11, 2022, from https://www.christianquotes.info/top-quotes/18-amazing-quotes-about-Gods-protection/.
2. NEEDS REFERENCE EITHER IN SENTENCE OR HERE
3. Tozer, A. W. (2020, September 24). *Quote by A. W. Tozer on the Shepherd and his sheep: Christian quotes of the day.* Christian Quotes of the Day | Daily Christian quotes to direct, inspire, encourage, and help ordinary Christians in the rough and tumble of their daily lives! Retrieved July 10, 2022, from https://christianquote.com/the-shepherd-and-his-sheep/.

Day 10

1. Stott, J. R. W. (2017, January 30). *Jesus Christ-death-substitution.* Grace Quotes. Retrieved July 9, 2022, from https://gracequotes.org/topic/jesus_christ-death-substitution/.

Day 11

1. Bounds, E. M. (2019, December 11). *Jesus Christ-death-cross.* Grace Quotes. Retrieved July 9, 2022, from https://gracequotes.org/topic/jesus_christ-death-cross/.

Day 12

1. MacArthur, J. (1999, July 11). *The Announcement of Jesus' Birth, Part 1.* Grace to You. Retrieved May 15, 2022, from https://www.gty.org/library/sermons-library/42-25/the-announcement-of-jesus-birth-part-1.
2. Edersheim, A. (1954). *Jesus the Messiah: Abridged edition of 'The Life and Times of Jesus the Messiah.* Eerdmans.
3. MacArthur.
4. Wangerin, W. (1999). *Preparing for Jesus: Meditations on the Coming of Christ, Advent, Christmas, and the Kingdom.* Zondervan.

Day 13

1. Longfellow, Henry Wadsworth, 1807-1882. Favorite Poems of Henry Wadsworth Longfellow. *Christmas Bells*. Garden City, N.Y. :Doubleday, 1947.
2. Harrell, Glenn, openhandspublications.com. (2019, December 24). *The Story Behind the Carol, "I Heard the Bells on Christmas Day"*. When Christmas is Just Hard to Do, Find Comfort in This Man's Story. Open Hands Publications. Retrieved May 15, 2022, from https://openhandspublications.com/2018/12/10/a-merry-christmas-say-the-children-but-that-is-no-more-for-me-escaping-the-doldrums/.
3. Ibid.

Day 14

1. Gladwell, Mary Beth, *The Shepherd Motif in the Old and New Testament*. The Shepherd Motif in the Old and New Testament | Dwell Community Church. (2021). Retrieved June 28, 2022, from https://dwellcc.org/learning/essays/shepherd-motif-old-and-new-testament.
2. BBC. (2005, July 8). *Turkish Sheep Die in 'Mass Jump'*. BBC News. Retrieved June 28, 2022, from http://news.bbc.co.uk/2/hi/europe/4665511.stm.
3. Challies, Tim. (2013, August 26). *Dumb, Directionless, Defenseless*. Challies.com. Retrieved July 28, 2022, from https://www.challies.com/christian-living/dumb-directionless-defenseless/.

Day 16

1. Lucado, Max. (2010). *Safe in the Shepherd's Arms: Hope and Encouragement from Psalm 23*. Thomas Nelson.
2. Hebrews 11:6.
3. Hill, E. V. (date unknown). *The Lord is My Shepherd*. Originally preached at the Mt. Zion Missionary Baptist Church. Los Angelos, CA. [Accessed by Cassette recording, June, 1993.
4. Psalm 23:4 (NIV). Emphasis added.

Day 17

1. Spurgeon, C. H. (June 28, 1877). *Until He Find It*. In https://www.spurgeon.org/resource-library/sermons/until-he-find-it/#flipbook/ (Vol.

49). Sermon, Metropolitan Tabernacle Pulpit. Retrieved July 1, 2022, from spurgeon.org.
2. John 10:27 (NIV).

Day 18

1. Pritchard, R. (2022, January 14). *December 3: Let's Go Straight to Bethlehem!* Keep Believing. Retrieved June 5, 2022, from https://www.keepbelieving.com/videos/december-3-lets-go-straight-to-bethlehem/
2. Dunn, M. (2018, December 9). *The Angels' Announcement.* Founders.org. Retrieved June 14, 2022, from https://founders.org/studies/ss-life-2018-12-23/
3. Luke 2:10.
4. Van Overloop, R. J. (2021, December 15). *Let Us Go to Bethlehem.* Protestant Reformed Churches in America. Retrieved August 7, 2022, from http://www.prca.org/resources/publications/articles/item/4547-let-us-go-to-bethlehem.

Day 19

1. Baldwin, James, 1924-1987. (1963). *Go Tell It on The Mountain..* New York: Dial Press.
2. Luke 2:10 (NIV).
3. Emphasis mine.
4. Motyer, J. A. (1993). *The Prophecy of Isaiah.* InterVarsity Press.

Day 20

1. Gilbert, Paul (2014). *The Sovereign Hand.* Steam Press.
2. Luke 2:17-18.
3. Spurgeon, Charles (2015). *"The Complete Works of C. H. Spurgeon, Volume 36: Sermons 2121-2181",* Delmarva Publications, Inc.

Day 21

1. Gordon, S. D. (1967). *Quiet Talks On Prayer.* Fleming H. Revell Co.

Day 22

1. Quotes, M. F. (n.d.). *Steven J. Lawson quotes: The high ground of Christ & Him crucified must be* ... More Famous Quotes. Retrieved July 6, 2022, from https://www.morefamousquotes.com/quotes/2083971-the-high-ground-of-christ-him-crucified.html.
2. Richard N. Longenecker, *The Expositor's Bible Commentary*, Volume 9, *John-Acts* (Grand Rapids, MI: Zondervan, 1981), p. 365.
3. R. Kent Hughes, *Acts: The Church Afire*, Preaching the Word (Wheaton, IL: Crossway Books, 1996), 120.

Day 23

1. David Platt, *Exalting Jesus in Matthew*, ed. Daniel L. Akin, David Platt, and Tony Merida, Christ-Centered Exposition Commentary (Nashville, TN: Holman Reference, 2013), Mt 9:37–10:42. Emphasis his.
2. Moore, B. (2020, February 10). *50 Christian quotes to inspire your faith every day*. Crosswalk.com. Retrieved July 21, 2022, from https://www.crosswalk.com/faith/spiritual-life/inspiring-quotes/30-inspiring-christian-quotes.html.

Day 24

1. Tony Evans, *Tony Evans' Book of Illustrations: Stories, Quotes, and Anecdotes from More than 30 Years of Preaching and Public Speaking* (Chicago, IL: Moody Publishers, 2009), 101.
2. Ivor Powell, *Matthew's Majestic Gospel*, Ivor Powell Commentary Series (Kregel Publications, 1986), 141–142

Day 25

1. Robert J. Morgan, *Nelson's Complete Book of Stories, Illustrations, and Quotes*, electronic ed. (Nashville: Thomas Nelson Publishers, 2000), 501.
2. Tom Wright, *Matthew for Everyone, Part 2: Chapters 16-28* (London: Society for Promoting Christian Knowledge, 2004), 141–142.

Day 26

1. Flavius Josephus, *The Wars of the Jews*, 6.9.3, *The Works of Josephus*, trans. William Whiston (Peabody, MA: Hendrickson, 1987), p. 749.
2. James Montgomery Boice, The Gospel of Matthew (Grand Rapids, MI: Baker Books, 2001), 549–550.
3. Leon Morris, *The Gospel according to Matthew*, The Pillar New Testament Commentary (Grand Rapids, MI; Leicester, England: W.B. Eerdmans; Inter-Varsity Press, 1992), 643–644.

Day 27

1. Piper, John. (n.d.). *Quotes about Jesus' death*. Quotes about Jesus Death (73 quotes). Retrieved July 12, 2022, from https://www.quotemaster.org/Jesus+Death.
2. Philip Graham Ryken and R. Kent Hughes, *Exodus: Saved for God's Glory* (Wheaton, IL: Crossway Books, 2005), 330.
3. Daniel L. Akin, *Exalting Jesus in Mark*, ed. Daniel L. Akin, David Platt, and Tony Merida, Christ-Centered Exposition Commentary (Nashville, TN: Holman Reference, 2014), Mk 14:12–16.

Day 28

1. Moody, D. L. (n.d.). *Quotes about Jesus' death*. Quotes about Jesus Death (73 quotes). Retrieved July 12, 2022, from https://www.quotemaster.org/Jesus+Death.
2. R. Kent Hughes, *John: That You May Believe*, Preaching the Word (Wheaton, IL: Crossway Books, 1999), 290.
3. Robert J. Morgan, *Then Sings My Soul Special Edition: 150 of the World's Greatest Hymns Stories* (Nashville: Thomas Nelson, 2010).
4. Ibid.

Day 29

1. Keller, Timothy. (n.d.). *Quotes about Jesus death*. Quotes about Jesus Death (73 quotes). Retrieved July 12, 2022, from https://www.quotemaster.org/Jesus+Death.
2. Flavius Josephus, *The Wars of the Jews*, 6.9.3, *The Works of Josephus*, trans. William Whiston (Peabody, MA: Hendrickson, 1987), p. 749.

3. James Montgomery Boice, *John*, Vol. 2 (Grand Rapids, MI:Zondervan, 1976), p. 219.

Day 30

1. Keller, T. (2015, August 10). *The story of the lamb – Timothy Keller [sermon]*.YouTube. Retrieved July 7, 2022, from https://www.youtube.com/watch?v=mY_cWXaovzg.

Day 31

1. Chan, F. (n.d.). *Top 100 quotes about Jesus' death: Famous quotes & sayings about Jesus' death*. Famous Quotes & Sayings. Retrieved July 12, 2022, from https://quotestats.com/topic/quotes-about-jesus-death/.
2. Mounce, B. (n.d.). *Bill Mounce*. The Aorist is so much more than a past tense. Retrieved July 18, 2022, from https://www.billmounce.com/monday-with-mounce/the-aorist-so-much-more-past-tense.

Day 32

1. Tozer, A. W., & Seaver, W. L. (2016). *Prayer: Communing with God in Everything--Collected Insights From A. W. Tozer*. Moody Publishers.
2. Karpenske, I., Platt, D. (2022, July 14). *Kindness That Leads to Repentance (Romans 2:4)*. Radical.net. Retrieved June 5, 2022, from https://radical.net/podcasts/pray-the-word/kindness-that-leads-to-repentance-romans-24/.

Day 33

1. Townend, Stuart, (1995) *How Deep the Father's Love for Us*. Thankyou Music.(PRS, admin. worldwide by EMI CMG Publishing).
2. John 3:16.
3. Lehman, Frederick Martin. (1917) *The Love of God*. Public Domain.

Day 34

1. Poole, William. (1907) *Just When I Need Him Most*. Public Domain.
2. Goodwyn, W. (2012, April 28). *Free After 25 years: A Tale of Murder and Injustice*. NPR.org. Retrieved July 1, 2022, from https://www.npr.org/

2012/04/28/150996459/free-after-25-years-a-tale-of-murder-and-injustice. Emphasis mine.
3. Genesis 39:2–3, 21, 23.
4. Psalm 34:18.

Day 35

1. Thrupp, Dorothy A. (1836) *Savior, Like a Shepherd Lead Us*. Public Domain.
2. Davis, Geron. (n.d.). *It Took a Lamb - lyrics and music by Geron and Becky Davis arranged by Gregbomia*. Smule. Retrieved July 21, 2022, from https://www. smule.com/song/geron-and-becky-davis-it-took-a-lamb-karaoke-lyrics/ 461647045_399239/arrangement.

Day 36

1. Burroughs, Dillon. (2012). *Hunger No More: A 1-Year Devotional Journey Through the Psalms*. New Hope Publishers.
2. Labott, E. (2021, July 22). *Get ready for a spike in global unrest*. foreignpolicy.com. Retrieved June 8, 2022, from https://foreignpolicy.com/2021/07/22/covid-global-unrest-political-upheaval/.
3. Keach, B. (1978). *Preaching from the Types and Metaphors of the Bible*. Kregel.

Day 37

1. Loock, D. (2022, June 29). *The Lion and the Lamb, Jesus Christ*. Open the Bible. Retrieved August 26, 2022, from https://openthebible.org/article/the-lion-and-the-lamb-jesus-christ/.
2. See Genesis 3:21.
3. Criswell, W. A. *(n.d.). The Scarlet Thread of the Bible*. Published with permission from the W. A. Criswell Foundation. *The Gospel Project. Retrieved July 5, 2022, from https://gospelproject.lifeway.com/wp-content/uploads/tgp2018/ 2018/04/The-Scarlet-Thread-Criswell.pdf.*
4. Wade, John Francis. (1841) *O Come All Ye Faithful*. Public Domain.

Day 38

1. Lewis, C. S. *(1950). The Last Battle* (Series: The Chronicles of Narnia). Macmillan.
2. Mendelssohn-Bartholdy, F., Trinity Choir, Dunlap, M., Marsh, L. I., Werrenrath, R. & Macdonough, H. *(1911) Hark! The Herald Angels*

Sing. [Audio] Retrieved from the Library of Congress, https://www.loc.gov/item/jukebox-130938/.
3. Watts, Isaac. (1719) *Joy to the World.* Public Domain.
4. Wesley, Charles (1739) *What Child is This.* Public Domain.
5. Stott, John R. (2006). *The Cross of Christ: 20th anniversary edition.* InterVarsity Press.

Day 39

1. Piper, J. (2018). *Don't Waste Your Life.* Crossway Books.
2. Kirvan, P. (2022, July 18). *What is Six Degrees of separation?* WhatIs.com. Retrieved August 10, 2022, from https://www.techtarget.com/whatis/definition/six-degrees-of-separation#:~:text=Six%20degrees%20of%20separation%20is,no%20more%20than%20five%20intermediaries.
3. Tom Ruprecht. (2001, December 6). *It's Actually Not a Small World.* McSweeney's Internet Tendency. Retrieved July 15, 2022, from https://www.mcsweeneys.net/articles/its-actually-not-a-small-world.
4. Isaiah 40:12.

Day 40

1. Romans 10:13 (NIV).
2. Kirkpatrick, William J. and Murray, James Ramsey. (1895) *Away in a Manger.* Public Domain. Emphasis mine.

Day 41

1. Davis, Geron. (n.d.). *Holy of Holies*-lyrics and music by Geron Davis. Arranged by Geron Davis and Bradley Knight. Publishing administered by Capitol CMG.
2. John 6:38.
3. Jones, M. (2015, April 2). *Christ's Death: His Willingness.* Reformation 21. Retrieved July 28, 2022, from https://www.reformation21.org/blogs/christs-death-his-willingness.php.

Made in United States
Orlando, FL
29 November 2022